ut of the car we
nd she will cry
We will say no. W
ut whenever she a
s and that our

Toni Morrison

ol has started, and Frieda and I get new brown stocking
er oil. Grown-ups talk in tired, edgy voices about Zick's
y and take us along in the evening to the railroad t
we fill burlap sacks with the tiny pieces of coal lying a
we walk home, glancing back to see the great carloads of
dumped, red hot and smoking, into the ravine that skirt
ill. The dying fire lights the sky with a dull orange
and I lag behind, staring at the patch of color surround
It is impossible not to feel a shiver when our feet leav
path and sink into the dead grass in the field.
house is old, cold, and green. At night a kerosene lamp l
ge room. The others are braced in darkness, peopled by r
mice. Adults do not talk to us -- they give us directions.
rders without providing information. When we trip and
hey glance at us; if we cut or bruise ourselves, they ask u
y. When we catch colds, they shake their heads in disgu
k of consideration. How, they ask us, do you expect anybo
ything done if you all are sick? We cannot answer them
s is treated with contempt, foul Black Draught, and casto
unts our minds.
, on a day after a trip to collect coal, I cough once, lo
bronchial tubes already packed tight with phlegm, my
ns. "Great Jesus. Get on in that bed. How many times do I
you to wear something on your head? You must be the bi
this town. Frieda? Get some rags and stuff that window
go by as quiet as lust, and drunken men and sober eyes
lobby of the Greek hotel. Rosemary Villanucci, our next
who lives above her father's cafe, sits in a 1939 Buick e
nd butter. She rolls down the window to tell my sister
that we can't come in. We stare at her, wanting her bread

Writers and Their Works

Toni Morrison

RICHARD ANDERSEN

Marshall Cavendish
Benchmark
New York

For Flore,
who made my house a home

With special thanks to Gayle Pemberton, professor
of English, African American Studies, and
American Studies at Wesleyan University, for
her expert review of this manuscript.

Marshall Cavendish Benchmark
99 White Plains Road
Tarrytown, NY 10591-9001
www.marshallcavendish.us

Library of Congress Cataloging-in-Publication Data
Andersen, Richard, 1946-
Toni Morrison / by Richard Andersen.
p. cm.—(Writers and their works)
Includes bibliographical references and index.
ISBN 0-7614-1945-4
1. Morrison, Toni. 2. Novelists, American—20th century—Biography.
3. African American novelists—Biography. 4. African Americans in literature.
I. Title. II. Series.
PS3563.O8749Z535 2005
813'.54—dc22
2004023757

Photo research by Linda Sykes Picture Research Inc., Hilton Head, SC

AP/Wide World Photos: 2, 19; Black River Historical Society: 6;
Lorain Public Library, Lorain, OH: 8, 10, 11; Bettmann/Corbis: 12, 16, 17, 30; Flip Schulke/Corbis:
14; Jacket illustration by Pascal Lemaitre (c) 2003, Simon & Schuster Inc.: 20 bottom; Landov: 20
top; (c) Houghton Mifflin Company, Boston, MA: 22; Jacket photograph: School Girl by Consuelo
Kanaga, 1963, The Brooklyn Museum. Gift of Wallace Putnam from the Estate of Consuelo Kanaga.
(c) Alfred A. Knopf, Publisher, New York: 24; Dick and Jane (c) 1946, 1940, 1956, Addison-Wesley
Educational Publishers, Inc./Grosset & Dunlap, Penguin Group (USA) Inc.: 53; Jacket design by
Wendell Minor (c)Alfred A. Knopf, Publisher, New York: 60; Library of Congress: 67;
Fundacion Collecion Thyssen-Bornemisza, Madrid, Spain/Art Resource, NY/VAGA: 112; Smithsonian
American Art Museum, Washington, DC/Art Resource, NY/VAGA: 119.

Printed in China
135642

Contents

THIS LORAIN (OHIO) HIGH SCHOOL YEARBOOK PHOTO, BELIEVED TO HAVE BEEN TAKEN IN 1945, IS OF THE YOUNG TONI MORRISON, THEN KNOWN AS CHLOE WOFFORD.

Chapter 1

How Toni Morrison Became Toni Morrison

> If anything I do, in the way of writing novels or whatever I write, isn't about the village or the community or you, then it isn't about anything. I'm not interested in indulging myself in some private exercise of my imagination . . . the work must be political.
>
> —Toni Morrison

STORIES. TONI MORRISON GREW UP ON STORIES. Lots of them and all kinds: gossip, legend, myth, folktales, family lore, even frightening ghost stories that would keep her awake at night. And everybody told them: grandparents, parents, and siblings. Had to. Never questioned why. Just told, listened, and enjoyed. And practically all the time. Every occasion, no matter how small, was an opportunity for someone in Morrison's family to tell a tale. Even her acceptance lecture when she became the first African American to win the Nobel Prize in Literature was a story.

Toni Morrison was born Chloe Anthony Wofford in Lorain, Ohio. Her dad George Wofford worked as a welder in a shipyard, but he also worked as a car washer, steel mill worker, road construction worker, and more. What Wofford did, he did well. Whenever he completed a perfect seam on any ship, he signed his name to it. And he passed on to his children his pride in perfection. To this day, Morrison continues to measure her accomplishments by what her father would approve of.

George Wofford was also a racist. Morrison often smiles when she uses the word "racist" to describe her dad, but she means what she says: "As a child in Georgia, he received shocking impressions of adult white people, and

TONI MORRISON'S FATHER, GEORGE WOFFORD, WORKED AS A WELDER IN A SHIPYARD WHEN SHE WAS A GIRL GROWING UP IN LORAIN, OHIO.

for the rest of his life felt he was justified in despising all whites, and that they were not justified in despising him."

Did her father's attitude toward whites influence Morrison? "Not when we were little," she tells us. "I knew he was wrong. I went to school with white children—they were my friends. There was no awe, no fear. Only later, when things got . . . sexual . . . did I see how clear the lines really were."

A religious woman who sang in her church's choir, Morrison's mother Ramah also struggled with racism. Though she believed that someday integration would be more than a dream, Ramah had "serious doubts about the quality and existence of white humanity." Meanwhile, she and her husband taught their children to rely on themselves, their family, and the black community.

What did George and Ramah Wofford mean by "rely on the black community"? Morrison describes her neighborhood in Lorain as a village in the African sense: "They felt that you belonged to them. And every woman on the street could raise everybody's child, and tell you exactly what to do, and you felt that connection with those people and they felt it with you. And when they punished us or hollered at us, it was, at the time, we thought, so inhibiting and so cruel, and it's only much later that you realize they were interested in you." Community in this sense of the word is the standard against which Morrison measures all the communities in her novels. In fact, Morrison's treatment of community—what it is, how it changes, and what it can change into—is as important to her as any of her characters.

One of the things by which a community is known is its stories: the myths, legends, and folklore that identify it, hold it together, and give it continuity. These kinds of stories were an integral part of her everyday life. Her grandmother kept a dream book that she used as a resource for playing the numbers, her parents and grandparents recounted family histories that could change depending on who was doing the telling, and her father told hair-raising ghost stories.

The children were also encouraged to tell stories of their own. It didn't matter if they were real or made up, if they included ghosts or talking animals. What was important, other than entertainment, was the truth that lay at the center of the story, the truth that was as real as any fact and often more so. "Without the belief in the supernatural," Morrison tells us, "I would have been dependent on so-called scientific data to explain hopelessly unscientific things."

In 1949, Morrison graduated with honors from Lorain High School, where literature was her favorite subject. She loved to read and couldn't get enough of anything written by Leo Tolstoy, Fyodor Dostoevsky, Gustave Flaubert, and Jane Austen. Especially Jane Austen. "Those books

LORAIN, OHIO, WAS AN INDUSTRIAL CENTER DURING MORRISON'S CHILDHOOD, INCLUDING FACTORIES SUCH AS THE NATIONAL TUBE COMPANY.

were not written for a little black girl in Lorain, Ohio, but they were so magnificently done that I got them anyway—they spoke directly to me out of their own specificity." Did Morrison ever think that someday her work would be compared with those of these authors? Did she even think about trying her hand at writing? "I wanted to be a dancer like Maria Tallchief, but when I wrote my first novel years later, I wanted to capture that same specificity about the nature and feeling of the culture I grew up in."

At Howard University in Washington, D.C., Morrison majored in English. She also began to think seriously about becoming a teacher. After receiving her Bachelor of Arts degree in 1953, Morrison enrolled at Cornell University in Ithaca, New York, where she wrote her master's thesis on the works of Virginia Woolf and William Faulkner. These writers may have influenced Morrison in two ways: Woolf encouraged women to write about the experiences they knew about better than men, and a central focus of Faulkner's work is his examination of power —who has it, how it is used, and how people respond to those who wield it.

Morrison's first teaching position after she graduated from Cornell was at Texas Southern University in Houston, one of only a few colleges that celebrated a "Negro history week." This event marked the first time

TONI MORRISON LOVED TO READ. SHE PASSED MANY HOURS IN THE LORAIN PUBLIC LIBRARY WHEN SHE WAS A GIRL.

TONI MORRISON EARNED HER BACHELOR'S DEGREE AT HOWARD UNIVERSITY IN WASHINGTON, D.C., AND, A FEW YEARS LATER, RETURNED TO TEACH LITERATURE AND WRITING.

Morrison thought about black culture as a discipline that could be formally studied like literature or history.

By 1957, Morrison was back at Howard University, introducing this new perspective to the students in her writing and literature classes. Two of those fortunate enough to know her then are the now famous literary scholar Houston Baker Jr. and Stokely Carmichael, the future Black Power leader of the 1960s who died in 1998.

An artist, for me, a black artist for me, is not a solitary person who has no responsibility to the community. It's a totally communal experience where I would feel unhappy if there was no controversy or no debate or no anything— no *passion* that accompanied the experience of the work. I want somebody to say amen!

—Toni Morrison

In 1958, Morrison met and wedded a young Jamaican architect named Harold Morrison. Their first son, Harold Ford, was born in 1961. You would think that teaching at a university, being married, and raising a child would be a dream come true, but Morrison has spoken of these years as being among the worst of her life: "I had no will, no judgment, no perspective, no power, no authority, no self—just this brutal sense of irony, melancholy, and a trembling respect for words."

To escape the unhappiness of her married life and find companionship with people who shared her love of words, Morrison joined a writers' group. Its members included LeRoi Jones, who would go on to become a famous poet, playwright, and political activist who changed his name to Amiri Baraka, and Claude Brown, who became widely known as the author of *Manchild in the Promised Land*. The group met regularly to read and critique each other's work. Too depressed to write,

ONE OF MORRISON'S STUDENTS AT HOWARD UNIVERSITY WAS
STOKELY CARMICHAEL, WHO BECAME A FAMOUS BLACK POWER
LEADER DURING THE 1960s.

Morrison read from essays she'd written in high school. One day, having run out of what she called "old junk," she wrote a story loosely based on a little black girl she knew as a child in Lorain. The girl used to pray that God would give her blue eyes. The group liked the story, and years later, Morrison would use it as the point from which to begin writing her first novel.

Unfortunately, whatever relief from marital pain Morrison found in her writers' group didn't last very long. By 1964, she'd left Howard University, divorced Harold, and returned to her parents' home with her son in tow and another baby on the way. Her second son, Slade Kevin, was born while Morrison lived in Lorain with no prospects in sight. She was down at the age of thirty but not out. And she wasn't down for long. Before the year ended, she agreed to take a job in Syracuse, New York, as an associate editor for a subsidiary of Random House. Still, it was "a terrible time," she told the television interviewer Charlie Rose. "Very hard. Awful." To the novelist Gloria Naylor, she said, "I was really in a corner. And whatever was being threatened by the circumstances in which I found myself, alone with two children in a town where I didn't know anybody, I knew I would not deliver my children a parent that was of no use to them. So I was thrown back, luckily, on the only thing I could depend on: my own resources."

She discovered she had more than a few to rely on. Morrison's family was at first dismayed and later awed that she could move to a place where she knew no one, work full-time at a highly demanding job, raise two children by herself, write in the evening after her two boys had been put to bed, and achieve such levels of success in her field that within two years she'd be promoted to senior editor at Random House headquarters in New York City.

And Morrison didn't stop once she hit the Big Apple. She didn't even slow down. Over the next twenty years, she would help more than twenty African-American authors

THE WRITINGS OF RADICAL POLITICAL ACTIVIST ANGELA DAVIS WERE EDITED BY TONI MORRISON WHEN SHE WAS A SENIOR EDITOR AT RANDOM HOUSE IN NEW YORK.

publish more than thirty-five books. These writers include Toni Cade Bambara, Gayl Jones, June Jordan, Angela Davis, Muhammad Ali, and Andrew Young, a former student from her writing group at Howard University and later the United States ambassador to the United Nations. But her most important early contribution as an editor may have been *The Black Book* of 1974. Her name isn't on the cover, but one of the ways we know she edited the book is that her parents are listed as a resource. A collection of materials from black history—newspaper clippings, photographs, soap advertisements, songs, bills of sale for slaves, recipes, rent-party jingles, maps to help slaves escape to the North, and more—*The Black Book* was produced at a time when many Americans felt the gains of the Civil Rights Movement in the 1960s were over. During

TONI MORRISON BROUGHT THE WRITINGS OF PROMINENT AFRICAN AMERICANS TO WORLD ATTENTION WHEN SHE WAS AN EDITOR. AMONG THE WRITERS WITH WHOM SHE WORKED WAS MUHAMMAD ALI, WHO BECAME THE WORLD HEAVYWEIGHT BOXING CHAMPION, AND AN ANTI-WAR ACTIVIST DURING THE VIETNAM WAR.

that time, the rhetoric of the Black Power Movement had deemed much of African-American culture to be of no use, reactionary, and too accommodating to white society. Morrison tells us she grew tired of reading histories about black life that focused only on its leaders. Determined to prevent the lives of everyday heroes from being reduced to a "lump of statistics," she created a history book that "recollected life as lived." A people's history.

As Morrison became the person most responsible for putting the stories of a lot of black women writers on the list of what students read in their literature classes today, many prestigious institutions sought her services. Between 1971 and 1972, she wrote a record twenty-eight reviews for *The New York Times Book Review* while also teaching at the State University of New York (SUNY) at Purchase. Invitations from Bard, Yale, and the University of California at Berkeley followed. So did a lot of honors. In 1977, President Jimmy Carter appointed Morrison to the National Council on the Arts; in 1981, she was elected to the American Academy of Arts and Letters; in 1984, she was named the Albert Schweitzer Professor of Humanities at the State University of New York (SUNY) at Albany; in 1989, she became the first black woman to sit in an endowed chair at an Ivy League college when Princeton University honored her as the Robert F. Goheen Professor of the Humanities; in 1993, she won the Nobel Prize in Literature; and in 1998, she served as the A. D. White Professor at Large at Cornell University.

These awards mark just the tip of her honors iceberg. None of them would have been possible, however, without the novels Morrison published between 1970 and 1998. The first of these books, *The Bluest Eye* (1970), shows how the dominant white culture's idea of beauty—blond hair, blue eyes, white skin—can turn self-esteem into self-hatred in the black community. In *Sula* (1973), Morrison presents a free-spirited character whose independent lifestyle is at odds with the black community in

TONI MORRISON ACCEPTED THE NOBEL PRIZE IN LITERATURE FROM KING CARL XVI OF SWEDEN ON DECEMBER 10, 1993. MORRISON WAS THE FIRST BLACK WOMAN— AND FIRST AFRICAN AMERICAN—TO RECEIVE THE AWARD.

TONI MORRISON'S YOUNGER SON SLADE HAS ALSO BECOME A WRITER. HERE, THEY ARE SIGNING COPIES OF *WHO'S GOT GAME?: THE ANT OR THE GRASSHOPPER?*, THE FIRST CHILDREN'S BOOK THEY WROTE TOGETHER. PICTURED BELOW IS ANOTHER BOOK WRITTEN BY MORRISON AND HER SON.

> Two people are busy making the story. One is me and one is you and together we do that, we invent it together and I just hold your hand while you're in the process of going there and hearing it and sharing it, and being appalled by this and amused by that and happy about this and chagrined about that and scared of this and grateful for that.
>
> —Toni Morrison

which she lives. Milkman Dead of *Song of Solomon* (1977) grows up in a community whose people are pressured to adopt the materialistic values of the white culture, but he doesn't want to give up the human qualities of his African-American heritage.

Tar Baby (1981) takes place on a Caribbean island where the traditional African-American resources of family and community don't exist. *Beloved* (1987), which won the Pulitzer Prize, is the story of an escaped slave who tries to kill her children rather than see them returned to a life of slavery. *Jazz* (1992) introduces two people who leave their small community in the South in the 1920s for life in a big city in the North, while *Paradise* (1998) tells the story of one black community's misguided attempts to recapture its past sense of purpose and being. In 2003, Morrison published *Love*, a novel about six women in love with a man who's still in love with a woman from his past.

We can see from these brief descriptions of her novels how important history is to Toni Morrison. But Morrison is not content to merely retell stories from the past. She also wants to refocus our perspective so the values of the people

> I think long and carefully about what my novels set out to do. They should clarify the roles that have become obscured; they ought to identify those things in the past that are useful and those things that are not; and they ought to give nourishment.
>
> —Toni Morrison

IN 2004, REMEMBER: THE JOURNEY TO SCHOOL INTEGRATION, WAS PUBLISHED. IN IT, MORRISON COMBINED ARCHIVAL PHOTOGRAPHS, HISTORICAL BACKGROUND, AND FICTIONAL NARRATIVE TO TELL THE STORY OF THE BLACK STUDENTS WHO WERE PIONEERS IN SCHOOL INTEGRATION.

who live the events she describes in her books can serve as sources of survival for people living today. In other words, she wants to keep the past alive by making it relevant to the present. Morrison's first two novels are about young people. Perhaps for this reason, they are the ones most often read by high school and college students. And though *The Bluest Eye* and *Sula* may be two very different coming-of-age stories, many critics see the second book as an outgrowth of the first. Let's discover what you think.

uns go by as quiet as lust, and drunken men and sober
g in the lobby of the Greek hotel. Rosemary Villanucci,
t-door friend who lives above her father's cafe, sits in a
ick eating bread and butter. She rolls down the window to
sister Frieda and me that we can't come in. We stare at

Book
OPRAH'S
Club

The Bluest Eye

Toni Morrison

Winner of the Nobel Prize in Literature

THE BLUEST EYE WAS TONI MORRISON'S FIRST NOVEL. IT TELLS THE
STORY OF A SELF-HATING AFRICAN-AMERICAN GIRL WHO WISHES SHE
WERE WHITE.

the lobby of the Greek hotel. Rosemary Villanucci, our n
r friend who lives above her father's cafe, sits in a
ick eating bread and butter. She rolls down the window to
sister Frieda and me that we can't come in. We stare at
nting her bread, but more than that wanting to poke the a
ce out of her eyes and smash the pride of ownership
ls her chewing mouth. When she comes out of the car we
t her up, make red marks on her white skin, and she wil
ask us do we want her to pull her pants down. We wil

Chapter 2

The Bluest Eye

> I wrote *Sula* and *The Bluest Eye* because they were books I had
> wanted to read. No one had written them yet, so I wrote them.
>
> —Toni Morrison

IF YOU HAD A HARD TIME TRYING TO FIGURE OUT what was
going on in *The Bluest Eye*, welcome to the club. The
unnumbered first chapter is only three paragraphs long, but
it is written in a kind of little kid's talk ("Here is the house. It
is green and white. It has a red door."). The second paragraph repeats the same words that make up the first paragraph,
only there is no punctuation and only one capital
letter ("Here is the house it is green and white it has a red
door"). The third paragraph repeats the words of the earlier
paragraphs but this time there are no spaces between the
words ("Hereisthehouseitisgreenandwhiteithasareddoor").
What's going on here?

Don't think you're going to find out in the second
chapter. It too is only three paragraphs long, but this time
the words are in italics and narrated by someone who's
obviously an adult determined not to clear up matters for
us anytime soon. Because the *"why"* is too difficult to
handle, this narrator tells us, she's going to focus on the
"how."

The third chapter is titled "Autumn." "Autumn" opens
with the line "Nuns go by as quiet as lust." Say what? Lust is
quiet? Like nuns? And that's just the beginning. In this chapter, the narrator is younger than the one in the second
chapter but not so young as to talk like the little kid in the
first chapter. And what does it mean that the margins in

this chapter are "ragged edged," while the margins in the previous two chapters are "justified"? The margins in the next two chapters are justified, but instead of being named after seasons, they're headed by excerpts from the third paragraph of the first chapter. Only now the letters instead of being small are all capitalized: "HEREISHOUSEITIS-GREENANDWHITEITHASAREDDOOR." Not only that, but the chapters headed by excerpts from the kid-talking section often contain stories told by characters in the novel. These stories within the larger story told by the narrator are in italics, but none of the stories in italics is told by the person who addresses us in italics in the book's second chapter. Is there no end to this confusion? Why is toni morrison doing this to us? doessheenjoymakingourlivesmiserable?

One way to approach the narrative difficulties of *The Bluest Eye* is to think about something else. Like the characters. If we can understand the characters, the ways they relate to one and other, and what Morrison is trying to say to us through them, we might be able to appreciate better the narrative package in which she places them and their actions.

The Characters

Pecola Breedlove and Claudia MacTeer. Pecola Breedlove is based on an African-American girl Morrison knew when she was growing up in Lorain, Ohio. Every night the girl asked God to give her blue eyes. But though the girl Morrison knew may have realized the absurdity of her request or possibly learned what inspired her to make it, Pecola literally drives herself crazy with her desire for a standard of beauty that undermines her self-esteem and causes her to hate herself. Not only doesn't she have blue eyes, she doesn't have straight hair or fair skin or a lot of other things that more than a few people mistakenly associate with beauty, virtue, and success.

If you've ever been upset with yourself because you don't look like a supermodel or an action hero, you have some idea of what Pecola is going through. One difference between you and Pecola, however, is that though you know that very few people can look like a model or an action hero without doing some serious physical and psychological damage to themselves, Pecola doesn't. She's still a child. And just about everything and everybody around her has been sending her the same message since she was a baby: Pecola, you are one ugly kid. Her mother, who also hates herself because she isn't white, started it. She thought Pecola was ugly on the day she was born, and by the time we meet Pecola in the novel, the poor girl is drinking as much milk as she can from a cup featuring Shirley Temple's image just to see the child star's "sweet" (read: "white") face.

The sad thing about all of this for both mother and daughter is they don't realize how much they hate themselves. They don't fully understand that most of the standards of beauty they aspire to are dangerous because they can make people who aren't white hate themselves. What Pecola and her mother do understand is that life for a white girl with blonde hair and blue eyes is a lot more pleasant than life for a black girl with black hair and brown eyes. And because they associate these physical traits of white people with qualities such as virtue, material comfort, and love, Pecola and her mother become victims of their own false values.

Psychologists call this condition "internalized racism" because the people who hate themselves aren't fully aware of it. That hatred has become so much a part of the way their minds work, they don't realize the damage they are doing to themselves. But the racism that eats away at their self-esteem often comes out in destructive behavior. They're aware of what they're doing, of course, but they don't know they are acting the way they do because the racist behavior of others has caused them to hate themselves. And the self-hatred they act out lowers their self-esteem even more. It often hurts others as well.

Let's take a look at one of the events in Pecola's life that has contributed to her hating herself because she's black. On her way to buy candy, Pecola stops to look at dandelions growing beneath a telephone pole and wonders why people call them weeds when they are so pretty.

When she arrives at Mr. Yacobowski's store, Pecola decides to spend her pennies on Mary Jane candy bars, but before she can get a word out of her mouth, she notices the way Mr. Yacobowski is looking at her. Or rather not looking at her because in his mind there is nothing of significance for him to see. He's not even curious to know what the little girl at his counter may want to buy. And what little emotion can be read in Mr. Yacobowski's eyes is distaste, the same distaste Pecola has seen in the eyes of other white people who have looked at her. When Mr. Yacobowski finally does talk to her, the tone of his voice confirms the look in his eyes. Pecola concludes without being aware of the damage she is doing to herself that this distaste must be because she is black. She can think of no other reason, and there is no other reason. Not in this case. Rather than find fault with the racist storeowner, however, Pecola unconsciously blames herself. If she wasn't black, Mr. Yacobowski wouldn't behave that way.

This idea that she is the one who is distasteful is reinforced in Pecola's mind when Mr. Yacobowski hesitates to take the money from her hand because he doesn't want to touch her black skin. Furious with herself for not looking like the kind of person worthy of Mr. Yacobowski's attention and respect, but not fully aware of why she's so upset, Pecola takes her anger out on the dandelions once she's left the store. "They *are* ugly," she tells herself. "They *are* weeds."

Pecola is conscious of what she is saying about the dandelions; what she doesn't realize is the underlying meaning of her message, the part that has been formed by the racism she has internalized within her psyche. That message reads: Since I can't be pretty, I'm not going to let the dandelions be pretty either. Releasing her anger with herself on the dandelions allows Pecola to feel a little better about her humiliation in the store, but the feeling lasts only until she remembers Mr. Yacobowski's blue eyes. That's when the shame of being black wells up inside of her again, and just before the tears come, she remembers the Mary Janes she bought with her three pennies.

The pale yellow wrapper for each candy bar has a picture of Mary Jane on it. A smiling white face, pretty blond hair, and brilliant blue eyes look out at Pecola from a world she imagines must be very different from her own: clean, comfortable, secure, and above all, loving. Pecola stuffs the candy into her mouth because in her mind to "eat the candy is somehow to eat the eyes, eat Mary Jane. Love Mary Jane. Be Mary Jane."

Now compare Pecola, whose name may come from a black girl who longed to be white in the 1934 film *Imitation of Life*, with her friend Claudia. Claudia hates Shirley Temple, but not because she has cute little dimples and curly hair and everybody loves her. She hates Shirley Temple because she gets to dance with Bojangles who, because he is black, Claudia sees as "*my* friend, *my* uncle, *my* daddy, who ought to have been soft-shoeing it and chuckling with me."

But Claudia's hatred for Shirley Temple isn't the first time she's reacted angrily against the impact of the white dominant culture. The first time is when her parents give her a little white doll as a Christmas present. The doll is supposed to make Claudia happy, but it does just the opposite. When she takes it to bed, the fingers scratch her skin, the head collides with her own, and the doll's eyes are "cold and stupid." Yet, her parents had told her the doll was beautiful.

PECOLA, THE MAIN CHARACTER IN *THE BLUEST EYE*, DRINKS MILK IN THE VAIN HOPE THAT IT WILL TURN HER AS WHITE AS SHIRLEY TEMPLE, THE CHILD STAR WHO WAS UNIVERSALLY ADORED FOR HER SWEETNESS.

Since Claudia can't see on its surface what's so special about the doll, she decides to investigate what's inside. She breaks off the doll's fingers, bends its feet, loosens its hair, twists its head, removes its eyeballs, and bangs its back against her brass bed rail until sawdust rains out, but no intrinsic quality worthy of adult adoration appears. The internal essence that Claudia doesn't even have a word for isn't there because it doesn't exist. What is there is a round disk with six holes that makes sounds like the icebox door opening in the kitchen of her home. Nevertheless, Claudia's mother tells her, "I-never-had-a-baby-doll-in-my-whole-life-and-used-to-cry-my-eyes-out-for-them. Now-you-got-one-a-beautiful-one-and-you-tear-it-up-what's-the-matter-with-you?"

Claudia doesn't know what's the matter with her. She's too young to understand her resistance to the way her family values the doll. Getting yelled at, however, is not the worst to happen to Claudia. That particular horror comes later when she realizes she's transferred her hatred for dolls onto little white girls. She tells us she wouldn't hesitate to axe any one of them if she thought she could discover the source of the magic they weave, the secret magic that makes adults say "Awwww" when they see little white girls but not when they see Claudia.

Pecola's parents: Pauline and Cholly Breedlove. Pauline Breedlove didn't grow up thinking she was ugly, but a slight limp caused by the infection from a rusty nail made her feel different from the time she was two. Restricted from playing with children, she found delight in order. She especially liked to arrange things—jars, sticks, stones, leaves—by lining them up in rows. By the time she was fifteen, she was taking care of her family's house single-handedly and dreaming of being swept away by a charming young "Presence" who would "lead her away to the sea, to the city, to the woods . . . forever."

Enter Cholly, who marries Pauline and leads her to downtown Lorain, Ohio, where he finds work in the steel mills and Pauline starts keeping house. But the people there see her as "country." She starts wearing make-up and tries replacing her Southern accent with a Northern one, but she can't find anyone who doesn't look down on her for being different. When she turns to her husband for companionship, he's initially supportive but before long is too busy getting drunk. The couple then starts fighting. Really fighting. Cholly uses his fists, feet, and teeth as weapons, while Pauline relies on heavier artillery, such as pots and pans. Most of their battles are over money. She spends too much and he never has enough. So she gets a job taking care of a white family's house. This satisfies her need for arranging things and maintaining order while waiting for the times when she and Cholly can make love. There aren't as many as there once were, but there are enough of them for Pauline to get pregnant twice. The first child is a boy named "Sammy"; the second is Pecola.

To counteract the loneliness she feels when she is home alone, Pauline starts going to the movies. It's the movies that do her in. Not only do they reawaken her ideas about romantic love, they introduce her to the concept of physical beauty. The narrator calls romantic love and physical beauty "the most destructive ideas in the history of human thought. Both originated in envy, thrived in insecurity, and ended in disillusion." It isn't long before Pauline begins equating beauty with virtue and measuring everyone she knows on a scale that has been created by images emanating from Hollywood. Poor Cholly isn't even close to Clark Gable (read: the Russell Crowe of Pauline's time).

But Pauline is no Julia Roberts either, especially after she breaks off her tooth on the candy she is chewing while watching a movie. That's when she turns to God. As a churchgoer, Pauline discovers she can suffer ugly Cholly like a "crown of thorns" and her ugly children like a "cross," and as the chief cook and cleaner in a well-to-do white family, she can satisfy her need to keep order. And be praised. The church provides Pauline with a community by which she's accepted, and the Fishers give her a home where she's appreciated. With its clean white sheets, comfortable furniture, and pretty blond children, the Fisher house is about as close as Pauline can get to the life she sees on the silver screen. No longer is she the Pauline of the kinky hair and missing tooth. She's not even "Pauline." Here her name is "Polly." Finally, she's been given a nickname—something she regretted not having as a child.

This psychic split between Pauline and Polly is graphically portrayed in the scene where Pecola spills her mom's freshly baked blueberry pie on the Fishers' kitchen floor. The burning juice from the pie splashes on Pecola's legs, and though the pain is terrible, Pauline/Polly can think only of the mess that's been made. She hits Pecola with the back of her hand, sending her sliding in pie juice across the floor; then she yanks her up by the arm, slaps her again, and tells her, "Crazy fool . . . my floor, mess . . . look what you . . . work . . . get on out . . . now that . . . crazy . . . my floor, my floor."

The angry and abusive tone in Pauline/Polly's voice changes, however, when she notices the blonde-haired, blue-eyed little Fisher girl upset over the juice that's stained her pretty pink dress. "Hush, baby, hush. Come here," she tells the child soothingly. "Don't cry no more. Polly will change it." No sooner are these words out of her mouth than Pauline/Polly turns her attention back to Pecola. "Get on out of here, so I can get this mess cleaned up," she spits at her daughter.

Pecola is only a few feet from the kitchen door when she overhears her mother further consoling the white girl:

"Don't worry none, baby."
"You gonna make another pie?"
"'Course, I will."
"Who were they, Polly?"
"Hush. Don't worry none," she whispered,
and the honey in her words complemented
the sundown spilling on the lake.

Imagine hearing your mom talk lovingly to some other kid in a voice you've never heard. Imagine Pecola having to call her mother "Mrs. Breedlove" while some white girl gets to call her "Polly." The central lesson of Pecola's life has once again been reinforced: in the world of the pink, white, and gold, she is ugly, unappreciated, and unloved. So is Pauline/Polly. She is so ashamed over the mess made by the blueberry pie, she can't bring herself to tell her employer's daughter who Pecola is. And not just because she's embarrassed by Pecola's behavior; she also doesn't want her white employers to know that anyone so ugly could be her daughter.

Cholly Breedlove's problems are worse. He was abandoned by his father before he was born and left to die by his mother in a trash heap when he was four days old. Rescued by his Aunt Jimmy and befriended by a kind old man named Blue, Cholly enjoys a stable, happy, loving life until he turns fourteen, Aunt Jimmy dies, and he meets a girl named Darlene at the funeral banquet.

Cholly and Darlene slip away from the banquet and are making love in an open field when Darlene suddenly freezes. Cholly thinks he's hurt her but then notices she is staring at two white hunters looming above them. One of the hunters pulls out a flashlight and tells Cholly, "Get on wid it, nigger." While Darlene covers her face in shame,

Cholly can only simulate what he'd been doing for real a few minutes before. "Come on, coon. Faster," one of the men tells him. As Cholly moves faster, his heart fills with hate not for the hunters but Darlene. He hates Darlene so much he wishes he could do what the hunters expect him to do and do it long, hard, and painfully. When the men leave, Cholly feels as if he wants to strangle Darlene but walks her back to the banquet instead.

For the next few days, all Cholly can think about is the white men, their flashlight, and Darlene covering her face with her hands. But instead of delivering a healthy dose of outrage against the hunters, Cholly directs his hostility toward the black girl who witnessed his inability to perform sexually. It then occurs to the inexperienced Cholly that Darlene might be pregnant. Even though this is biologically impossible, the thought inspires the boy to track down his father in Macon, Georgia, to see if the old man will take him in.

Taking the twenty-three dollars Aunt Jimmy had hidden in an unused stove flue, Cholly tries to buy a train ticket for a child twelve years old or younger. The stationmaster isn't fooled. "I reckon I knows a lying nigger when I sees one," the stationmaster tells the boy, but he gives Cholly a ticket just in case there's some truth to the claim that he's going to see his dying mother. This man is in the same racist league as Mr. Yacobowski, but unlike Mr. Yacobowski, he is given a redeeming quality: Underneath all his revolting rhetoric is a decent human gesture. We can't condemn him quite as thoroughly as we did the prejudiced storeowner.

Almost miraculously, Cholly finds his father in Macon, and almost predictably, loses him within minutes. Before Cholly can even say his name, his father dismisses him with a barrage of cruel words about the boy's mother. Cholly is too stunned to respond. The best he can do is collapse on a nearby orange crate until the strength comes back in his legs. Straining to keep from crying over the loss of his aunt and his father's rejection, he defecates in his pants. What's he going to do now? What if his father sees him? Afraid of the laughter that would ring in his ears, Cholly runs to a pier jutting out from the Ocmulgee River. He crouches behind one of the posts, and without bothering to clean himself, curls into a fetal position, covers his eyes with his fists, and falls asleep.

When water appears in a story or a painting or a movie, it's almost always a sign that some kind of dramatic change is going to take place. The person in the story, painting, or movie is going to go into that water and come out a changed person. Or perhaps when we see the depicted character, he or she has already come out of the water. It doesn't matter which side of the water the person is on; the message is almost always the same: rebirth.

The next morning, Cholly cleans his underwear and trousers in the Ocmulgee River and emerges a free man. Dangerously free. Because he has nothing left to lose, Cholly no longer has to answer to anyone but himself. For the first time in his life he is alone. Really alone. And being really alone, he is the only one of any interest to him.

It is in this state of dangerous freedom—dangerous because it lacks any sense of responsibility—that Cholly meets Pauline Williams and, feeling empowered by the joy he is able to awaken in her, marries her. The limited, constant routine of marriage, however, drives Cholly to despair, and he starts doing to his wife what he would like to have done to the white hunters. Eventually, he finds whatever comfort he can in a bottle of alcohol.

The appearance of two children in Cholly's life only makes matters worse. Because of what's happened to him in his life, he has no idea how to love Sammy and Pecola. So instead of understanding and perhaps treating them as he should, he reacts, and his reactions are based on whatever he happens to be feeling at the time. It is in this dangerous state—drunk, free, irresponsible, and living in the moment—that Cholly comes upon his eleven-year-old daughter washing dishes.

Cholly's first reaction to Pecola's presence is a cross between pity and revulsion. Her hunched back, her head leaning constantly to one side, and her overall sense of helplessness and hopelessness make him feel sorry for her. But the idea that he might be partially responsible for Pecola's condition and that she loves him in spite of himself makes Cholly want to break her neck—but gently. How dare she love him and put him in the position of having to return it. Return it how? He'd never accepted her love in the first place. The very idea of loving and being loved makes Cholly want to vomit, but before the sensation in his stomach can make its way to the kitchen floor, Pecola stands on one foot to scratch the back of her calf with her toe. This gesture is the same one Pauline was making when Cholly first laid eyes on her. It fills him with a kind of pity for himself and a gentle lust for his daughter. Here's how Morrison's narrator describes what happens next: "He closed his eyes, letting his fingers dig into her waist. The rigidness of her shocked body, the silence of her stunned throat, was better than Pauline's easy laughter had been. The confused mixture of his memories of Pauline and the doing of a wild and forbidden thing excited him, and a bolt of desire ran down his genitals, giving it length, and softening the lips of his anus." Cholly wants to rape his daughter, but he wants to do it "tenderly."

Cholly's so-called tenderness quickly evaporates, and his subsequent violent act evokes Pecola's only response: "a hollow suck of air in the back of her throat. Like the rapid loss of air from a circus balloon." By the time Cholly has had his way with her, the girl has fainted. But Daddy isn't quite through. His mixed feelings of hatred and tenderness return. The former prevents him from picking his daughter up from the floor; the latter inspires him to cover her with a quilt.

Incest and rape are not easy subjects to talk about. What Cholly does is so horrible, it's hard to look past it. But looking past Cholly's rape of Pecola is exactly what Morrison wants us to do. By making him a sympathetic character—abandoned, emasculated, rejected—she tries to prevent us from seeing him as a villain. He may be confused, scarred, and disturbed, but he is not evil. With no parents to nurture him into adulthood, no community to protect him from racism, and without a job to enable him to adequately support his family, he is a victim as well as a victimizer.

He's also something of a romantic figure. In an interview with Robert Stepto, Morrison says she sees Cholly's freedom as a symbol of "the tremendous possibility for masculinity among black men." They may be unemployed or in prison, but they have a sense of adventure about them, a kind of "magic and feistiness that nobody has been able to wipe out." Fine, but what happens when these men wipe out others? What about those, like Cholly, who've learned that to be a man is to oppress others the way the white hunters and his father have oppressed him? What share of the responsibility is his and how much belongs to the environment from which he comes? We may not be able to condemn Cholly totally, but is Morrison telling us he should be exonerated for his terrible violation of Pecola and perhaps even admired for his adventuresome spirit?

This is a difficult question to answer. Morrison doesn't allow Cholly to get away with his crime—he dies later in a workhouse—but she presents the rape scene solely from his point of view. And in an article entitled "Unspeakable Things Unspoken: The Afro-American Presence in American Literature," Morrison claims she feminizes Cholly's masculine act. It is "passive," she says, "and, I think, more accurately repellent when deprived of the male 'glamour of shame' rape is (or once was) routinely given." This is certainly true. Morrison's sensitive treatment of Cholly has enabled her to create one of the most exquisitely rendered and painful-to-read scenes in all of American literature.

Claudia's Parents: Mr. and Mrs. MacTeer. Mr. and Mrs. MacTeer contrast with Pauline and Cholly Breedlove in ways that parallel the contrast between Claudia and Pecola. Like the Breedloves, the MacTeers are poor. They light their living room with a kerosene lamp, fear the mice and roaches that hide in the darkness, and require their children to search the railroad tracks for pieces of coal. Mr. MacTeer works long and hard to support his family, and though Mrs. MacTeer seems to enjoy complaining, she's dedicated to her home and family. Like many over-worked parents, they talk to their two children more than they listen, but they also take care of the kids and fill their home with a love that Claudia tells us is as thick and as dark as syrup: "And in the night, when my coughing was dry and tough, feet padded into the room, hands repinned the flannel, readjusted the quilt, and rested a moment on my forehead."

The MacTeers also have a sense of responsibility to the people in their community. When, before raping his daughter, Cholly Breedlove set fire to his house, beat his wife, and got his family put "outdoors," the MacTeers allowed Pecola to live with them in spite of the extra burden they knew she would create. Mrs. MacTeer may have complained about the new girl's drinking three quarts of milk, but her anger is directed toward her irresponsible parents, not the child: "Folks just dump they children off on you and go on 'bout they business. Ain't nobody even *peeped* in here to see whether that child has a loaf of bread. Look like they would just *peep* in to see whether I had a loaf of bread to give her. But naw. That thought don't cross they mind." Ironically, it is Pauline Breedlove who sees herself as a martyr, and Mrs. MacTeer who makes the sacrifices.

Irony: "Irony" means saying the opposite of what you mean. When someone spills something on you and you say, "Great! Nice shot! Just what this shirt needed!" you're being ironic. But in literature, irony is often expressed not in specific words but in how a character acts or a plot is developed. That Pauline thinks she's a martyr while it is Mrs. MacTeer who makes all the sacrifices is ironic. The sight of Pecola picking through the trash in a Dumpster at the end of the novel becomes ironic when we remember her father being left in one when he was four days old.

Fortunately for Claudia and her sister Frieda, Mrs. MacTeer sings almost as much as she complains. She also differs from Pauline Breedlove in other ways. There's no room for self-pity in her life, she's not hung up on being beautiful, and she won't allow anything to stop her from fulfilling her duties as a parent. The same can be said of Mr. MacTeer, who works day and night to keep his family fed, clothed, and sheltered. And did you notice that Mr. MacTeer is the only man in the novel not hostile to women? Inspired by Morrison's father, Mr. MacTeer goes so far as to throw his tenant off the porch when he suspects the man of having touched Frieda's breasts.

Geraldine and her son Junior. Geraldine, like Pauline Breedlove, aspires to what she thinks is the norm in the white dominant culture: perfumed bodies, manicured lawns, and well-furnished houses. But to gain what she sees as a privileged status, she thinks she has to erase all traces of being black. Trying to be what she is not (white) and hating what she is (black), Geraldine turns her back on her people and her culture and focuses on what she can control: her house, her husband, her son, and herself.

Geraldine's story starts in a place that is somewhere between rural and urban. All the men are employed, and all the women use well-known commercial products. To smell and look a certain way is a big part of what they think it means to be "respectable."

Like many girls who want to improve their circumstances, Geraldine goes to college to learn how to teach black children to be obedient rather than think for themselves. She develops good manners, high morals, and a ruthless passion for eliminating "funk" wherever she sees it. Which happens to be just about everywhere: in too loud a laugh, too grand a gesture, too much sway in a walk. Identifying, controlling, and eliminating funk wherever and whenever it shows its ugly head may be a lifelong battle, but each victory provides Geraldine with the order and constancy she needs to reinforce the image of herself as clean, respectable, and virtuous.

When Geraldine and her husband make love, she often wonders why people's private parts couldn't have been put in a more convenient place, such as the palms of their hands. After they have sex, she heads to the bathroom with relief. Repressing the erotic and passionate in her life is another way for Geraldine to protect herself from the funk. It also gives her a sense of power over her husband and whatever funk he might still possess. If only her cat could be her husband! Her cat, which is as clean and as quiet as she, is funkless.

And so is her son. He doesn't get as much affection as the cat, but Geraldine sees that he's always brushed and bathed, plays only with white kids, and knows the difference between "colored people" and "niggers." Colored people are clean and quiet like him and his mother; niggers are dirty and loud like his friend Bay Boy. As he grows older, Junior starts hating his mother for placing so many restrictions on him. But because she is bigger and stronger, he redirects his hatred onto her innocent cat and children who are smaller and weaker than he. Most of these children are girls.

Like Pecola. Junior sees her walking alone and invites

her to play with the kittens he claims have recently been born in his house. She is so excited by the lace doilies, potted plants, white lampshades, and images of flowers in a rug she almost forgets why she's there. "Here is your kitten," Junior reminds her as he throws his mother's cat in Pecola's surprised face. "You're my prisoner," he then tells the girl and leaps out of the room to hold the door shut and prevent her from leaving. Pecola starts crying but becomes distracted by the cat, whose eyes are blue. When Junior doesn't hear any more sobs coming from the room, he bursts in, grabs the cat by one of its hind legs, and swings it around his head in a cruel display of anger against what he correctly sees as the only recipient of the little love his mother possesses. Pecola tries to stop him, but Junior manages to fling the cat at full force against a window. The poor animal, a victim of Geraldine's failure to nurture her son in childhood, slithers down behind a radiator and stays there.

Enter Geraldine. She sees Pecola's dress, now torn from her struggle with Junior; her hair, now matted where the plaits have come undone; and her muddy shoes with the wad of bubble gum sticking out between the soles. Funk has somehow managed to get in her house. Funk is threatening to disturb the order and pattern of her life. Funk is reminding her of who she really is.

"She killed your cat," Junior tells his mother. In a voice that echoes that of Cholly's father when he rejected his son in Macon and foreshadows what Pecola will hear from her own mother in the Fishers' kitchen, Geraldine tells Pecola: "Get out of my house."

Order and tranquility are restored, but at what cost? By defining herself through her ability to repress the funk she associates with black people, Geraldine's life is stilted; by insisting on a perfection she associates with whites, her son becomes dangerous; and by measuring her worth by victories over whatever threatens her value system, she has victimized and scarred an innocent child.

Maureen Peal. Through Maureen Peal, we witness another type of prejudice that can exist among members of the same race. It's called "colorism," and it has to do with African Americans whose skin is lighter than those of other African Americans. These light-skinned African Americans are often given privileges by both whites and blacks because their skin is closer to the standard of beauty that's so frequently touted in the popular culture. But the reverse is also true. Many dark-skinned African Americans discriminate against light-skinned African Americans because they are not "pure."

Maureen is a new girl in the school attended by Pecola, Claudia, and her sister Frieda. A "high-yellow dream child" with "sloe green eyes" and straight brown hair, she also comes from some money. She wears patent-leather shoes and fluffy sweaters, and her rabbit fur coat has a matching muff. Her teachers encourage her in class, her schoolmates treat her with respect, and she never has to search for someone to sit next to in the cafeteria. Frieda and Claudia try to find flaws in her, but they can't come up with much. They turn her name into "Meringue Pie," discover she has a "dog tooth," and smile in small triumph when they see she's had a sixth finger removed from each of her hands.

One day on their way home from school, the three girls come across some boys harassing the one girl in all of Lorain, Ohio, who is probably the complete opposite of Maureen: Pecola. "Black e mo. Black e mo," they chant as they dance around her in a macabre ballet. "Ya dadd sleeps nekked. Black e mo." Is there no end to what this poor girl must endure? How is she going to respond to this? The boys, who are unaware of the racism that has infected their senses of self, are also black. Driven by contempt for themselves, they direct their feelings of inferiority against a girl who has no defense and for whom they have no respect. Unlike Maureen, Pecola is "black e mo"; she is ugly.

And what is Pecola to make of the accusation that her father sleeps naked? Don't these boys have a father among them who sleeps with no clothes on? What are they saying? In the end, it doesn't matter because they get what they want: Pecola drops her notebook and covers her eyes with her hands as the boys gaily circle about her and bombard her with their cruel taunts.

Frieda and Claudia rush to their friend's rescue, but the boys are reluctant to back away until Maureen appears at Claudia's elbow. Their solidarity broken by the new girl's presence, they drift off, and Maureen puts her arm through Pecola's in a gesture of friendship. The four girls walk on with Claudia becoming increasingly annoyed at Maureen, especially for treating Pecola to an ice cream cone and not offering to buy cones for her and Frieda. When Maureen asks Pecola if she's ever seen a naked man, Claudia has had all she can take. She starts arguing with Maureen, but the light-skinned girl pulls rank: "And you ugly!" she tells the sisters. "Black and ugly black e mos. I am cute." Claudia and Frieda retaliate with "Six-finger-dog-tooth-meringue-pie," but their words don't have much bite: "Maureen Peal was not the Enemy and not worthy of such intense hatred," Claudia realizes. "The *Thing* to fear was the *Thing* that made *her* beautiful, and not us."

China, Poland, and Miss Marie the Maginot Line. Infernal Triad or Holy Trinity? These happy whores, as their names suggest, are larger-than-life characters, and they better be if they plan to hold the line of free-spiritedness against the Geraldines, Paulines, and Maureens of the world. Or at least of Lorain, Ohio. "Whores in whores' clothing," they defy all stereotypes.

They also have a special place in their hearts for Pecola. Their home is in the same building as hers, but they live on the floor above and light-years away from the hate and squalor that's bred in her parents' apartment.

Pecola loves visiting China, Poland, and the Maginot Line because she always feels welcome there. They may be bursting with funk, but because their interests extend beyond property and propriety and they haven't lost their senses of humor, they serve as an example of some of the ways people can be decent, caring, and supportive. For this reason, they invite comparison with the community of women Pecola's father knew as a child in Georgia. When Cholly's Aunt Jimmy is taken seriously ill, women from her neighborhood try to nurse her back to health, and when Aunt Jimmy dies, the women prepare her body, arrange her funeral, and help find a home for Cholly.

Now compare these two communities of concerned, nurturing women with the women in Lorain who talk about Pecola after she's been impregnated by her father. Listen to the tone in their voices:

"Well, they ought to take her out of school."
"Ought to. She carry some of the blame."
"Oh, come on. She ain't but twelve or so."
"Yeah. But you never know. How come she didn't fight him?"
"Maybe she did."
"Yeah? You never know."
"Well, it probably won't live. They say the way her mama beat her she lucky to be alive herself."
"She be lucky if it don't live. Bound to be the ugliest thing walking."

How could these women possibly think a twelve-year-old girl could be partially responsible for her father's raping her? These women and others like them show shock, disgust, amusement, and outrage at what's happened to Pecola, but none of them reveal so much as an ounce of pity for her. Claudia and her sister listen for the woman who will say, "Poor little girl" or "Poor baby," but the words never come. Why not? Because people like Pecola make people like the women in Lorain feel better about themselves. They cannot derive a sense of beauty from the dominant culture, so they beautify themselves by making others ugly. They may be poor, they may have husbands who beat them, they may have to do work for white people that should be doing the work for themselves, but as bad as their lives are, they're not as bad as Pecola's. The farther down on their scale of respectability that they can put people like Pecola, the higher up they can place themselves. It's not bad enough she's been raped by her father; she should be taken out of school because of the bad example she sets for the other children.

The Maginot Line. Named after the French Minister of War, this huge system of fortifications along the French-German border was supposed to protect France from German aggression after World War I. Its heavy guns could turn in only three directions so they could never be fired on France. So what did the German Chancellor Adolf Hitler do at the outset of World War II? He had his troops flown over the Maginot Line so they could attack it from its virtually defenseless rear. German troops were in Paris in a matter of weeks. Why do you think Toni Morrison called one of her three whores "The Maginot Line"? Could it be because Pecola was attacked in ways the Maginot Line couldn't defend?

Looking up to the white standard while looking down at people like the Breedloves creates a tension between poor blacks and those who are better off. Because many middle-class blacks think poor blacks make them look bad in the eyes of the white dominant culture, they resent and hate poor blacks. These women of Lorain demonstrate how this kind of thinking works. They'd like to take their hostility out on Cholly, but they're afraid to because Cholly might set their houses on fire. So they choose as their victims the weakest of the weak. The farther they can push poor Pecola toward the bottom of the community's social barrel, the closer they can raise their own senses of self-worth to the top. Or as close to the top as they think they can get. You can measure the insecurity of these women by the extent of their cruelty. The crueler they are, the more insecure they are; the more they are threatened, the crueler they become.

Soaphead Church. Different from the other characters in *The Bluest Eye* because his self-image has been (de)formed by the racism that stems not from slavery but from colonization, Soaphead is able to trace his lineage back to a decaying British nobleman named Sir Whitcomb. Soaphead's nineteenth-century ancestors learned and taught those who came after them all there was to know about separating themselves in body, mind, and spirit from anything that suggested Africa. "Marrying up," they lightened their complexions, altered their features, and stood out among their peers in school. Soaphead, known on his island in the Caribbean as Elihue Micah Whitcomb, learned his lessons of self-hatred and became an expert in the art of self-deception. At seventeen, he met Velma, who left him two months after they were married because he associated lovemaking with Holy Communion.

It was the beginning of the end for Elihue. He entered the seminary on his island but was never ordained; he moved to the United States but couldn't handle the study of psychiatry. He then embarked on a downward spiral that began with a job as a desk clerk in a "colored" hotel in Chicago and bottomed out in Lorain, Ohio, where he passed himself off as a minister. Unlike so many immigrants from the Caribbean who have suffered discrimination at the hands of African Americans, however, Elihue found success. His accent, his celibacy, his fastidiousness, and the odd way he used soap to keep his hair in place made him seem supernatural rather than unnatural. People came to him for advice, and he discovered a marketing niche in their fear.

By the time Pecola knocks on his door, Soaphead has convinced himself that all imperfection is God's fault, and his mission is to correct his maker's shortcomings. Of course, Soaphead doesn't see either his pedophilia or his hatred of his landlady's mangy dog Bob as shortcomings.

Soaphead invites the noticeably pregnant Pecola into his home, learns she's been kicked out of school, and finds her request for blue eyes perfectly understandable. Unaware of the self-hatred inscribed on his psyche by the white supremacist values he's internalized, Soaphead would like to grant the girl's wish, but he's no magician. He's not above taking advantage of the superstitious, however, and seeing Bob on his landlady's back porch, he envisions a scheme in which Pecola will kill the unfortunate dog. Telling the girl he's only an instrument of God's will and her desire for blue eyes is totally up to him, he gives her some meat he's poisoned and tells her to feed it to Bob. If the dog acts strangely, she'll know her prayers have been answered.

Bob dies horribly, Pecola flees in horror, and Soaphead immediately explains his behavior in a letter to God. He didn't do what he did for money, and he didn't do it for sex. "I did what You did not, could not, would not do," he exults. "I looked at that ugly little black girl, and I loved her. I played You. And it was a very good show!"

Actually, it was a pretty poor one. An insecure shell of a man who has nothing better to do than vent his frustrations on a defenseless dog and an innocent child, Soaphead doesn't care what damage he does or to whom as long as he satisfies his enormous ego.

The Community. *The Bluest Eye* is more than just a story about a girl who's driven mad by her desire to attain a false standard of beauty. Pecola wasn't born with this desire; she learned it from the people who made her feel worthless. Her story is also the story of a community that persecutes its weakest members. With the exception of the MacTeers, none of Lorain's residents step forward to help the Breedloves. It is also only a MacTeer who feels any sense of responsibility for what happened to Pecola. Claudia says:

> All of us—all who knew her—felt so wholesome after we cleaned ourselves on her. We were so beautiful when we stood astride her ugliness. Her simplicity decorated us, her guilt sanctified us, her pain made us glow with health, her awkwardness made us think we had a sense of humor. Her inarticulateness made us believe we were eloquent. Her poverty kept us generous. Even her waking dreams we used—to silence our own nightmares. And she let us, and thereby deserved our contempt. We honed our egos on her, padded our characters with her frailty, and yawned in the fantasy of our strength.

The Narrative Structure

It's so carefully done, it can practically be diagrammed. Pecola is at the center because this is her story. All the other major characters serve to reflect, explain, or in some other way comment on what happens to her, and they fall into two main groups. The first group is made up of people who contribute to Pecola's going insane. This group includes her hate-breeding parents, the repressed Geraldine and her aggressive son Junior, the light-skinned Maureen, the racist storeowner Mr. Yacobowski, the self-hating boys in the playground, and the fraudulent minister of gullible souls Soaphead Church. The second group of characters comprises those who present alternative role models for Pecola—Mr. and Mrs. MacTeer and the three happy whores—as well as those who also try to protect Pecola from the community's need to turn her into a scapegoat—the MacTeer sisters. Claudia tells us, "I wanted to open her up, crisp her edges, ram a stick down that hunched and curving spine, force her to stand erect and spit the misery out on the streets. But she held it in where it could lap up into her eyes."

Scapegoating. In biblical times, the high priest would symbolically lay the sins of the people on a goat, and the goat would be driven from the community. You can read about this ancient practice in Leviticus 16: 8–22.

Even more impressive than the way she balances the characters around Pecola is how Morrison uses the "Dick and Jane" story that opens the novel. For decades, practically all American children were taught to read from books that told stories about a family of four that was white, middle-class, and happy. The kids' names were Dick and Jane. Everyone in the family had blond hair and blue eyes and all their problems were little ones. These books also taught children a lot more than how to read. The kids learned that happiness depended on a father who went to work in a suit and tie, a mother who stayed home, a refrigerator that was always full, and a lawn that never grew weeds.

The Bluest Eye opens with an artificial, contrived, perfect word picture that begins: "Here is the house. It is green and white. It has a red door. It is very pretty. Here is the family. Mother, Father, Dick and Jane live in the green and white house. They are very happy." In the next paragraph, Morrison repeats the first paragraph only without any punctuation, and the only capital letter is the one that begins the first word: "Here is the house it is green and white it has a red door." In the third paragraph, there are no spaces between the words: "Hereisthehouseitisgreenandwhiteithasareddoor." Why do you think Morrison decided to do this? Why couldn't she be satisfied with just telling the story the first way?

A simple answer to these two questions is that she may be thinking of the story as a symbol of what can happen to people who keep hearing the same message over and over again. Pauline, Geraldine, Soaphead, and Pecola have been hearing these words (and others like them) for so long they not only can't get away from them, they've all been neurotically damaged by the never-ending message that "black is ugly e mo."

Another reason why Morrison has presented these three paragraphs these three ways may be to demonstrate how we learn to internalize behavior. When we as children read that opening paragraph from the "Dick and Jane" story for the first time, it took a while. We had to sound out each letter before we realized what the words meant. We needed the periods and the capital letters to tell us when to stop and when to go. But as we read the story more and more, the reading became easier and the speed with which we read became faster. We almost didn't need the periods, or at least we weren't conscious of looking at them. When called on to read aloud in class, no one ever said, "Here is the house period." By the time we became thoroughly familiar with the story through repetition, we didn't have to read any sentence word-for-word to understand it. We could scan the words very quickly and still know their meaning because we'd become so familiar with the action and the characters. It wasn't long before we could look at a whole page and know what it was about as soon as our eyes landed on a few important words: "house," "Dick and Jane," "dog," etc. We really knew that story! What we didn't know was the extent to which we were also internalizing its subliminal message about what was attractive in the dominant culture and what was not.

One of the most creative ways of looking at the Dick and Jane story is to see the three versions as symbols of a community that believes and passes on to others the false values of the dominant culture. The first version of the story, the one that's written the way we're used to seeing words in print, is what the white dominant culture has established as the standard against which everyone is measured. This is not only the way respectable middle-class people are supposed to look and live, it is also the way they are supposed to write. Anyone who doesn't look, live, and write according to the standard is considered inferior. And those who don't reach this standard are punished by those who have because, if they don't maintain the standard, they will lose power.

The second version of the Dick and Jane story is almost the same. It retains spacing between the words but contains no punctuation. This version symbolizes those characters in the novel who want to be like the people in the Dick and Jane story but can't get there. Think of Geraldine and Soaphead, who think they can be respectable by eliminating the blackness in their lives.

The third version, the one with no punctuation and no spaces between the words, represents those who are farthest away from reaching the norm but still try. Pauline and Pecola are two examples. Only those not caught up in this hierarchy of power—the MacTeers, the three whores, and the women who take care of Cholly's Aunt Jimmy—are free of it. Cholly may be free of it too, but his is a dangerous freedom because it's irresponsible. And look what happens to him: He sets fire to his house, rapes his daughter, gets sent to a workhouse, and dies.

Morrison reinforces her point about what the three versions of the Dick and Jane story symbolize by using

Storybook Treasury of

Dick and Jane
and Friends

FOR MANY YEARS, AMERICAN CHILDREN WERE TAUGHT TO READ FROM DICK AND JANE PRIMERS, WHOSE SUBLIMINAL MESSAGE WAS THAT A "GOOD" FAMILY WAS WHITE, BLAND, AND WELL-DRESSED. MORRISON TURNS THAT NOTION ON ITS HEAD IN *THE BLUEST EYE*.

phrases from the story to introduce some of the chapters within the novel. The first time she does this is when she wants to contrast where the Breedloves live with the standard that has been established by the Dick and Jane text. This chapter opens with the section from the children's book that reads, "HEREISTHEHOUSEITISGREENITHASAREDDOOR-ITISVERYPRETTY." The Breedloves do not measure up very well. To begin with, their "house" is a storefront: "Visitors who drive to this tiny town wonder why it has not been torn down, while pedestrians, who are residents of the neighborhood, simply look away when they pass it."

The next time Morrison uses an excerpt from the Dick and Jane story is when she wants to introduce the people who live in the storefront: "HEREISTHEFAMILYMOTHER-FATHERDICKANDJANE." The parents are always fighting, the son is always running away, and the daughter is always obsessing about blue eyes: *"Pretty eyes. Pretty blue eyes. Big blue pretty eyes. Run, Jip, run. Jip runs, Alice runs. Alice has blue eyes. Jerry has blue eyes. Jerry runs. Alice runs. They run with their blue eyes."* Did you notice that the simple structures of Pecola's sentences are almost identical to those in the Dick and Jane story? Why do you think Morrison did this?

The three happy whores living on the second floor of the storefront contrast with the Breedloves' ugly ways, but they also contrast with the lack of emotion apparent in the people represented in the Dick and Jane text. Could it be that underneath the gleaming surface of pretty blond hair, happy blue eyes, and clean, orderly homes, life is rigid and cold? If they're all so perfect, why doesn't anybody want to play with Jane? The father smiles, the mother laughs, the cat meows, the dog barks, and Jane has to find a playmate outside the family.

The chapter on Geraldine, who loves her cat at the expense of her son, is introduced by the cat lines in the Dick and Jane story, and the chapter on Soaphead, the dog who kills Bob, is headed by the dog lines. Also,

Geraldine and Soaphead are the only middle-class blacks in the novel. What do you make of this? Is Toni Morrison having some fun with the structure of her narrative, or is she symbolically telling us something significant? Is it possible to do both at the same time?

There's no question about the serious, foreboding statement Morrison makes when she introduces the chapter in which Cholly rapes his daughter: "SEEFATHERHEIS-BIGANDSTRONGFATHERWILLYOUPLAYWITHJANE." Knowing what's going to happen, the irony is almost too much to bear. He may try to rape her "tenderly," but he'll never understand or even be aware of the self-hate he continually turns against Pecola, Pauline, and himself. And nothing he does satisfies it. He can't hit Pauline often enough, and he even tried to rape Pecola a second time.

The Dick and Jane texts demonstrate Morrison's ability to turn form into content. First, she uses the story to show us how the standards of the dominant group establish a hierarchy of power. Those who look, live, and write like the narrator of the Dick and Jane text have power in the dominant culture; those who don't look, live, and write like the narrator of the Dick and Jane text do not. Having power means having more control over your life. The more control you have over your life, the better your chances of being happy. If you want the happiness that you think comes with neat, orderly homes and well-manicured lawns, you have to conform to the standards that are being imposed upon by you by the dominant culture. If you don't conform, you're punished.

But Morrison doesn't begin every chapter with an excerpt from the Dick and Jane story; four chapters begin with the names of the seasons. In each of the chapters labeled after the seasons, Claudia speaks to us from the first-person viewpoint of a nine-year-old child: "I was going to miss something. Again. Here was something important, and I had to stay behind. . . ." She tells us in these chapters what she sees as the important events in Pecola's childhood, especially the first time she had her period: "That night, in bed, the three of us lay still. We were full of awe and respect for Pecola. Lying next to a real person who was really ministratin' was somehow sacred." All of the chapters that are introduced by the seasons and are told to us by nine-year-old Claudia have "ragged-edged" margins. The margins of the chapters that begin with excerpts from the Dick and Jane story are all "justified." And while the chapters with the seasons are narrated from the first-person point of view of a child, the chapters where the margins are justified are narrated from the objective, authoritative viewpoint of an adult. Once again, form becomes content. Claudia's youthful perspective, narrated in her own speaking voice, is necessarily "ragged"; she can't at her age understand what she will as an adult. Looking back at these events from the viewpoint of an adult, however, she writes in a voice that is more carefully constructed. She can now "justify" what was only "ragged" in her mind as a child. She? If you haven't already guessed, all the chapters are written by Claudia. The ones that are labeled by the names of the seasons are written by Claudia as a child; the ones headed by excerpts from the Dick and Jane story are written by Claudia the adult. But Morrison doesn't make that clear until the last chapter when the third person point of view ("A little black girl yearns for the blue eyes of a little white girl. . . .") shifts to first person ("We saw her sometimes. Frieda and I—after the baby came too soon and died.").

Within one of the chapters—told by the adult Claudia using justified margins—is a story told in the first person and printed in italics. This is Pauline Breedlove's story, and she tells it in her own voice from her own point of view. So in this chapter, the one that begins "SEEMOTHER-MOTHERISVERYNICE," you have Claudia telling us from her third-person point of view about Cholly and Pauline, and you have Pauline telling us about herself from her own first-person point of view. To make the reading of these chapters easier for us, Morrison puts what Pauline has to say in italics: *"Cholly was thin then, with real light eyes. He used to whistle, and when I heerd him, shivers come on my skin."* Check out whether Pauline's story has ragged or justified edges and think about why Morrison made the choice she did.

The chapters headed by the names of the seasons are presented in this order: autumn, winter, spring, summer. Why? One reason may be that they are told by the child Claudia, and the new year for most kids is when school begins in September. Another is what happens in each of the seasons to the characters in the novel. In the fall of 1940, Cholly sets his house on fire and Pecola goes to live with the MacTeers. Everything deteriorates quickly from this point on. That winter, the kids in the playground torment Pecola, and Geraldine confirms their view that Pecola is "black e mo" when she drives the girl from her house. Spring for Pecola is even bleaker than winter. Her mother kicks her out of the Fisher house and, in a chapter that comes before the one entitled "Summer," her father rapes her. That Cholly's rape occurs during a season of rebirth is as bitterly ironic as his washing his soiled clothes in the Ocmulgee River and coming out a changed but not an improved man. Summer can't come soon enough for the oppressed in Lorain, Ohio, but it doesn't make anything better.

Claudia and Frieda, in a childlike twist of logic, plant some marigold seeds too late in the hope of saving Pecola's baby. In the fall of 1941, one year after Claudia began her story, the seeds fail to sprout, and Pecola's baby dies. Interestingly, Morrison places the news about the seeds and Pecola's baby not at the end of the novel in chronological time but at the beginning. The book's second chapter opens in the fall of 1941; the third chapter takes place in the fall of 1940. When neither the marigolds nor the baby survive, the sisters blame each other for the way the seeds were planted. Years later, they come to realize that the ground in which they planted the seeds, like the barren life that exists in the Breedloves' home and the community of Lorain, was barren. Nothing can be grown where nothing can be cultivated: the seeds, Pecola's baby, and the sisters' innocence all die in the fall of 1941.

The Title

We know from some of the characters in *The Bluest Eye* that Morrison didn't find their names in a telephone directory. "Cholly and Pauline Breedlove," the couple incapable of breeding love, are obvious examples of how Morrison sometimes uses names to convey meaning. "Maureen," "Pauline," and "Geraldine" may rhyme because they're all in the same self-hating boat. But what about *The Bluest Eye*? Shouldn't the title be *The Bluest Eyes*? Not only does Pecola pray for more than one eye, but hers are not the only blue eyes in the novel. The racist storeowner Mr. Yacobowski has a pair and so does Geraldine's cat. Given Morrison's concern with names, the title couldn't be an oversight.

Could the one eye symbolize those who internalize the limited views of the white dominant culture? If so, its gaze permeates all the way down to the colonized citizens of Lorain, who "see" Pecola as "ruined" because she is no longer "respectable." Her position solidified in childhood as the village pariah, Pecola is reduced as an adult to going through garbage for a living. And Claudia tells us that because Pecola allowed the community to diminish her, she deserves its contempt. Think about that for a minute. Pecola is the victim, and yet it's her fault for letting the people of Lorain victimize her. Wow! Claudia may have written her way out of her own subjugation, but do you think she still might have a way to go as far as the subjugation of others is concerned? At the very last page of her story, she's still holding on to the illusion that Cholly loved his daughter. "I'm sure he did," she tells us. "He, at any rate, was the one who loved her enough to touch her, envelop her, give something of himself to her." Has Claudia forgotten or perhaps dismissed the fact that he raped Pecola senseless, left her on the floor with only a quilt to protect her from the wrath of her mother, impregnated her with a child that she would lose but not before getting kicked out of school, and then tried to rape her again? And what about Pecola's having what was left of her fragile spirit raped by Soaphead and forced to find refuge in insanity from critical eyes of the black community? With fathers like Cholly, Pecola doesn't need enemies.

When Pecola looked into a mirror as a child and didn't see anything remotely resembling what she'd been taught she needed to look like if she wanted to be beautiful and loved, a gap was created between her and the standard represented by blue eyes. So she tried to bridge this gap by, among other things, pigging out on Mary Jane candy bars. We know, however, that such a wide gap can never be bridged, and Pecola will always be ugly in any mirror held up to her by those who've internalized the racist standards of the dominant culture. In the insanity that allowed her to see the world as it should be seen, however, Pecola refused to accept the impossibility of her quest, and in a pathetic twist of imagination, created her own mirror, a friend who would tell her as often as needed that her eyes are more beautiful than anybody's.

Want to impress your teacher? Refer to *The Bluest Eye* as a *Bildungsroman*. A *Bildungsroman* is a fancy word for "growing-up story." English majors say it all the time. The word is pronounced just like it sounds except for the last few letters. Instead of saying "man" the way you ordinarily would, say "mahn." What's interesting about Toni Morrison's *Bildungsroman* is that while Claudia grows up, Pecola grows down.

Pecola's destruction isn't total —she is alive at the end of the novel and her imaginary friend does provide some sense of self-worth—but it could hardly be much worse. This may be Pecola's story, but it is Claudia we must look to for hope as a model of the pride and anger needed not only to survive but triumph over the fate of individuals and communities whose senses of self are negated by a dominant culture.

SULA

A novel by TONI MORRISON

SULA IS ABOUT THE FRIENDSHIP OF WOMEN, AND ABOUT A BLACK
WOMAN WHO REFUSES TO TOE THE LINE

Chapter 3

Sula

I was certainly interested in talking about black girlhood in *The Bluest Eye* and not so interested in it in *Sula*. I want to move it into the other part of their life. That is, what do the Claudias and Friedas, those feisty little girls, grow up to be?

—Toni Morrison

SULA ISN'T *THE BLUEST EYE II*, but the territory is strikingly familiar. So is the way Morrison guides us through it. Remember how the two girls are contrasted in the earlier novel and how all the other characters either help drive Pecola insane or, like Claudia, treat her with respect? Morrison uses the same technique in *Sula*, only this time the two girls at the center of the novel don't become friends until they are adolescents, but the girls' parents contrast almost as markedly as the Breedloves and the MacTeers.

Most of the action in *Sula* takes place in Medallion, a small Ohio town that is not unlike Lorain, and there's a trip to Louisiana that echoes in structure Cholly's search for his father in Georgia. Both novels contain a house run by three women, a confrontation between innocent girls and abusive boys, a community that acts like a character, a fellow called "Shadrack" whose name sounds too much like "Soaphead" to be coincidental, and numerous self-hating African Americans.

The themes haven't changed much either. Morrrison continues to explore in *Sula* the effects of history and racism: those of the white dominant culture on the black community and those of the black community on its own members. The virtues of nurture and support are once again pitted against the vices that result from poverty and racism, and the line separating "good" from "bad" behavior is often disturbingly thin. As in *The Bluest Eye*, those who do seemingly bad things can neither be completely condemned nor totally exonerated, but those in *Sula* who act in the name of good may not have that right. Sometimes people do wrong things for right reasons, and sometimes they do right things for wrong reasons.

Symbols also abound. Remember the marigolds in *The Bluest Eye*? In *Sula*, it's the robins that die. Water plays a bigger role in *Sula* than it did in *The Bluest Eye*, but all but one of the rebirths are equally unsuccessful. Names like "Peace" and "Wright" in *Sula* comment on the characters that go by them in much the same way as "Breedlove"—the family that breeds hate—and "Maginot Line"—the prostitute who holds the line against conventional morality—contribute to our understanding of those people in *The Bluest Eye*. The grotesque is also here: A woman who cuts off her leg to save her children can't save her daughter from burning to death as an adult because she doesn't have a leg to stand on.

Victims and victimizers are well represented too. Remember the character in *The Bluest Eye* who was so "free" he never felt an impulse to be responsible? He's baaaaack. Only this time he's a she and not nearly as dangerous. No children get raped in *Sula*.

One difference between the two novels is the packaging. Whereas *The Bluest Eye* is a relatively simple story placed in a complicated structure, *Sula* is a more complicated story placed in a relatively simple narrative form. It may begin with an ending and end with a beginning, but there's no outside text like the Dick and Jane story to start us off confused, and the chapters follow a chronological time line from 1919 to 1965. All the pages have justified margins, no one talks in italics, all the words are separated by spaces, and the narrator who speaks mostly from the third person point of view is not one of the two girls at the novel's center now grown up. Let's start our discussion of the novel with those two girls.

The Characters

Sula Peace and Nel Wright. Sula cannot have Peace without (W)right, and Wright cannot be (W)right without Peace. Two halves of a whole, Sula is impulsive and imaginative, while Nel is reasonable and reserved.

Nel's house looks as if it was decorated by Geraldine from *The Bluest Eye*. Dick and Jane would love it! Everything is always clean and neatly arranged, but Nel never feels comfortable there unless Sula is with her. Sula, on the other hand, loves Nel's house because it's so different from her own. There are no newspapers stacked in the hallway and no dirty dishes left for hours in the sink, but neither is there something always cooking on the stove or someone dropping by unexpectedly. Which is why Nel prefers Sula's home to her own. Each girl is attracted to what the other has, and each has qualities the other lacks.

When we first meet Nel, she is a child about to travel with her mother Helene to New Orleans to see her mother's dying grandmother. Helene Wright, like Pauline of the *The Bluest Eye*, is a member of her town's most conservative black church and enjoys the sense of power that comes from manipulating her husband and child. Helene also has a beautiful new dress to make herself feel better on a train bound for the Deep South.

Unfortunately, Helene doesn't get as far as Cincinnati before her defenses come under attack, and she starts to crumble the minute a white conductor addresses her as "gal." Nel has never seen anybody be disrespectful to her mother. When Helene explains she walked into the "whites only" car by mistake, the conductor tells her, "We don't 'low no mistakes on this train." Pointing to the adjoining car for "colored only," he continues, "Now git your butt on in there."

Helene responds in a way Nel has never seen. Like a dog that wags its tail at the person who's kicked him just minutes before, Helene smiles foolishly and coquettishly at the conductor who's insulted her. Nel can see from the stricken faces of two black soldiers in the next car how disgusted they are by her mother's response, and she's embarrassed. But she's also pleased when neither of the soldiers helps her mom put her bags in the overhead luggage rack. Mrs. Helene Wright of Medallion, Ohio, Nell concludes, is not the intimidating figure she pretends to be. Underneath all her pride, elegance, and ability to dominate with no more than a look, she is of little more substance than "custard."

But if her mom is made of custard, isn't there a good chance Nel might be too? This thought inspires little Nel to make a big promise to herself: No man will ever look at her the way the soldiers looked at her mother. She also takes a long, hard look in the mirror once she's back at home. Staring at the brown eyes, braided hair, and broad nose her mother despises, Nel tells herself: "I'm me. I'm not their daughter. I'm not Nel. I'm me. Me."

Enter Sula. Sula and Nel have been going to the same school for five years, but they've never played together because Nel's mom told her Sula's mom was "sooty." Now that she's "Me," Nel can't think of a better reason for getting to know Sula. To say the two hit it off is an understatement. "Their friendship was as intense as it was sudden," the narrator tells us. "Daughters of distant mothers and incomprehensible fathers . . . they found in each other's eyes the intimacy they were looking for."

The girls share everything from ice cream to dreams of romance, but there are some important differences.

Friendship between women is not a suitable topic for a book. Hamlet can have a friend, and Achilles can have one, but women don't, because the world knows that women don't choose each other's acquaintanceship. They choose men first, then women as second choice. But I have made women the focal point of books in order to find out what women's friendships are really all about.

—Toni Morrison

One of these can be seen in the way each views the arrival of her future Prince Charming. While Nel pictures herself passively waiting with tangled hair on a bed of flowers, Sula sees herself riding a horse in full view of someone who likes to move at high speeds.

Three important childhood events bond the girls forever. The first of these occurs when they are twelve, and they find themselves harassed by four Irish teenagers every day on their way home from school. The sons of immigrants resented for swelling the labor pool and depressing wages, they re-direct the hate that's been inflicted on them toward the small and weak. In this sense, they are not much different than the self-hating boys in *The Bluest Eye* who taunt and torment Pecola in the playground on her way home from school.

One day the Irish boys discover Nel by herself and push her from one to the other until they grow bored with looking at her frightened and helpless face. The girls take a longer way home for the next few weeks, but come November, Sula has had it with cold weather and insists that she and Nel take a shorter route. When the boys see Nel and Sula walking down the street, they can't wait to take out their frustrations on the two girls. Sula's pulling a paring knife excites them even more. Now they don't have to pretend to be engaging in innocent fun; now they have the excuse they need to indulge in some real violence. But before they can lay a hand on the girls, Sula cuts off the tip of her left forefinger. The boys are stunned. "If I can do that to myself," Sula tells them, "what you suppose I'll do to you?" End of confrontation.

As "blood sisters," the girls explore whatever strikes their fancy: one-eyed chickens, sheets flapping in the wind, and comments from the boys they pass hanging out at the local pool hall. They have no priorities, but there are some changes. Nel no longer wears a clothespin at night to straighten her nose, and although she still has to suffer her mother's hot comb, straight hair no longer interests her. Sula's attitude toward her family shifts when, on her way to the bathroom before heading to a nearby river with Nel, she overhears her mother Hannah tell a friend, "I love Sula. I just don't like her." The words sting, but Sula can't take time to think them through because her friend is calling her to participate in what will be their second important bonding experience.

The girls run most of the way to the river and lie down under a canopy of trees. Swept up by the wildness that has risen within them, their heads almost touching, they engage in an activity that is so sexually charged it has led some critics to conclude that Nel and Sula are latent lesbians. The scene begins with the two girls stroking blades of grass without looking into each other's eyes. Not consciously aware that they are stroking phallic symbols, they move on to peeling the bark from two twigs, stripping them to a "smooth, creamy innocence." Once the twigs are "undressed," Nel tears up some grass to make a place where she and Sula can draw patterns on the ground. The patterns quickly turn into two holes as the girls move from creating designs to poking their twigs "rhythmically and intensely" into the earth. Eventually, the two holes become one impression and Nel's twig breaks. When she throws her broken phallic symbol into the hole, Sula does the same with her twig. They then fill the hole with scraps of paper, bits of glass, and butts of cigarettes before covering the "entire grave" with grass.

We have no pictures of the fictional *Sula*, but she might
have looked and dressed something like this.

What have the girls buried? Twigs and trash or something of much larger significance?

Morrison denies that Nel and Sula are lesbians. In an interview with Nellie McKay, she points out their clear and intense preoccupation with men and claims that the critics who think her characters are gay aren't familiar with "the culture, the world, the given quality out of which I write." Could it be that the critics who interpret *Sula* as a story about lesbians might be jumping too quickly to a conclusion that furthers their own social and political agendas? Houston Baker Jr., the Albert Greenfield Professor of Human Relations at the University of Pennsylvania, thinks so. He argues that to build the case for a lesbian reading on a few scenes and the words that describe them is almost comical because it ignores just about everything else in the novel. Yes, Nel and Sula adore each other; yes, they accept each other uncritically; and yes, their relationship is sexually charged, but their relationship isn't any more charged than that of many girls on the brink of their first sexual encounters; many young people accept each other uncritically, and lots of adults, both heterosexual and homosexual, adore each other.

Now for the third bonding experience. After burying their phallic symbols (?) in the vaginal opening (?) they turn into a grave (?), the girls are joined by Chicken Little. Nel yells at the boy for eating whatever he can find in his nose, but Sula encourages him to climb a nearby tree. Chicken Little is a little chicken at first, but with Sula's help, he manages to climb high enough to see farther than he has ever seen. When they get back to the ground, Sula grabs the boy by his wrists and swings him in a circle. Round and round they go, faster and faster, until the girl loses her grip, the boy flies into the river, and the water closes over him. Chicken Little doesn't surface, but neither do the girls try to rescue him.

Are they in shock? Perhaps. But they're not so shocked

they fail to notice someone who might have seen them. It's Shadrack, the town's resident eccentric, who urinates in front of women and gets away with cursing white people. Sula runs to his cabin. She's so surprised to discover how neat and clean it is she almost forgets why she's there, which is amazing when you consider she's just killed an innocent child. Suddenly, she discovers Shadrack looking at her. Nodding his head as if he were answering a question, he tells her, "Always."

Sula runs back to where Nel is waiting for her and collapses in tears. Nel assures her friend that what happened isn't her fault. Sula cries again at the funeral and Nel expects the sheriff to show up at any moment, but Chicken Little is laid to rest without incident. At the cemetery, the girls hold hands at a distance from the gravesite, and the narrator tells us both girls know Chicken Little's coffin is all that's going in the earth; his bubbly laughter will haunt them "forever."

These scenes—confronting the Irish boys, burying the twigs, and allowing Chicken Little to drown—show some of the ways Nel and Sula bond by complementing each other. When Nel fears the boys, Sula defends her. When the girls ritualistically peel and bury the twigs together, each responds to the other's movements without any words being exchanged. Their friendship is so close, "they themselves had difficulty distinguishing one's thoughts from the other's." When Sula is hysterical over Chicken Little's death, Nel calms her down by assuring her she's not responsible. There's a symbolic as well as actual gap between Sula and Nel while they're sitting in the pew at Chicken Little's funeral, but that gap closes once the boy is buried and they're standing together at the cemetery. Now the gap is between the girls and the gravesite.

The two girls leave the burial relaxed, their hands clasped gently. The narrator says the press of Chicken Little's fingers in the palm will forever be above ground, but the girls behave like "any two young girlfriends trotting up the road on a summer day wondering what happened to butterflies in the winter." Does this behavior contradict what the narrator said earlier about the horrible memory living forever in the girls' minds? Shouldn't they be more upset? Or are they too young to realize the significance of what they've done? Or is the girls' relaxed behavior a cover for the dark secret they will always share? Whichever way(s) you think makes the most sense, Nel and Sula use Chicken Little's death to bond more solidly with one another.

These bonding scenes are important for another reason. As much as the girls share the same dreams, develop the same notions of sexuality, resist the excesses in each other's houses, and carry within them the secret of Chicken Little, the way they respond to these events reveals a fundamental difference in Nel's and Sula's psychological makeup. Nel, for all her talk about "Me," is still more rational, conventional, and passive than Sula. Nel is the one who prefers to avoid the Irish bullies, admonishes Chicken Little for eating snot, sits on the ground while he and Sula climb the tree, watches while Sula swings the boy in a circle, waits while Sula runs to Shadrack's house, and convinces Sula she's not responsible for Chicken's death. It's Sula, on the other hand, who cuts off the tip of her finger, climbs the tree with Chicken Little, sends him flying into the river, confronts Shadrack in his cabin, and cries hysterically at the river and again at the funeral. But Sula is not just more impulsive, more confident, more emotional, more willing to take risks, and more prone to violence than her friend. She also has a tendency to go overboard. Her cutting off the tip of her own finger is almost insanely disproportionate to the threat posed by the Irish bullies. Where did she learn to think, act, and demonstrate love this way?

From her family. Much of their behavior is markedly

unconventional. Lore has it that Sula's grandmother Eva cut off her leg to collect the money she needed to support her three children from an insurance policy. One of these children, Sula's mother Hannah, engages in frequent sexual activity because she likes to be touched every day by men. Standing up or sitting down, in the pantry or on the floor, it doesn't matter how, when, or where, as long as it's not in bed. In bed, the men might fall asleep. In Hannah's mind, sleeping with a man in her bed is a sign of intimacy, and intimacy is not what sex is about.

Never scolded, never given directions, and never encouraged to sustain a thought for more than three minutes, Sula grows up in a home that has no room for the word "ordinary." This is why she needs Nel. Nel's calming consistency in the eye of a storm, her regard for the well-being of others, and her ability to keep things in perspective, balance Sula's wilder, more imaginative side. Nel, as her last name suggests, makes things (W)right. Nevertheless, Nel needs Sula as a haven to whom she can go to escape her mother's pressure to conform to the dictates of conventional behavior. When Nel is with Sula, she can be "Me." In other words, each girl lacks some quality the other has. There's one lack in Sula, however, that Nel can't compensate. She doesn't even know about it. When Sula overhears her mother telling a friend that she "loves" her daughter, but doesn't "like" her, the girl's psyche is seriously affected.

Then there's Sula's reaction to Chicken Little's death. She cries at the river and at the funeral, but again says nothing to Nel to indicate any guilt, remorse, responsibility, or even concern about the possible consequences of her behavior. Could the reason be that she may not be crying so much for Chicken Little as for herself? The narrator tells us: "The first experience taught her there was no other that you could count on; the second that there was no self to count on either." These are disturbing thoughts for anyone, let alone a twelve-year-old. If Sula can't count on herself or anyone else, what does that make Nel? What does that make Sula?

Chicken Little may be the one who goes into the river, but it is Sula who experiences a rebirth. She emerges from the event a free woman in much the same way that Cholly becomes a free man after he washes his soiled clothes in the Ocmulgee River. Dangerously free. Freed from any obligation to the mother who doesn't love her, Sula frees herself from any responsibility in the death of the innocent boy. That she probably shouldn't have been swinging Chicken Little so close to the river or that she should have stopped swinging him when she felt her grip on his wrists weaken never seems to have entered her head. How do we know Sula didn't release her grip just so she could see what would happen? How do we know Sula, who shows no hesitation to act quickly and dramatically in every other situation we've seen her in, didn't rush to rescue Chicken Little because she was curious to see someone drown? How do we know that when the two girls walk hand in hand down that road after the boy is laid to rest, they aren't also laying to rest their own emotional maturity? Even rational, responsible Nel never suggests or, so far as we know, even considers reporting what happened to her parents or some other adult authority. Could it be the increased bonding that comes with keeping their secret to themselves is more important? What does that say about their love? A comment by the narrator in another context may also apply here: "In the safe harbor of each other's company they could afford to abandon the ways of other people and concentrate on their own perceptions of things."

Five years go by before we next see the two girls together. The occasion is the wedding reception of Nel and Jude Greene. Nel wasn't all that interested in marrying handsome, likable Jude when he talked about getting work on the new road and tunnel that would connect

Medallion with towns across the river, but when the construction company hired "skinny white boys" over him and she saw how badly he'd been hurt by the blatant racism, he became more attractive to her. Soothing Jude's pain made her feel good. In fact, the more he hurt, the more she cared for him, and the more she cared for him, the better she felt about herself. We can see what's happened. Nel has become more like her conventional mother than she would have thought possible when she was a child, especially after vowing to be "Me." She isn't haughty or mean-spirited like Helene, but she has come to see herself in terms usually associated with those of traditional wives and mothers.

There's also more to this part of the story than may at first meet the eye. Jude is a victim of racism. Deprived of economic opportunity and the social advancement that often comes with it, African Americans have had to find alternative ways of surviving. One of these ways is by pulling together, by making individual sacrifices for the good of a larger whole. This whole ranges from families to people in the neighborhood to the communities in which black people live. For the sake of his family, Jude is willing to work longer hours in his job at the hotel to make up for what he's not given the opportunity to earn in the construction industry; Nel is willing to sacrifice the independence she finds in her relationship with Sula to enjoy the appreciation that comes with building a family. This appreciation comes not only from Jude, who takes care of Nel and makes her feel beautiful, but from the community whose survival depends in large part on its female members' willingness to conform to certain proscribed norms. These norms include letting the man in the family be the man he's not allowed to be in the workforce, sacrificing your own development as a human being for your children's future, and realizing that your image of yourself as a woman depends more on how the community sees you than on how you see yourself.

What Nel, her mother Helene, and the many women who think like them don't often realize is that sacrificing individual fulfillment for the well-being of others can come at a higher personal cost than they may be aware of at first. These women may survive for a while in their homes but they rarely succeed outside them because their worlds are no longer their own once they marry. On the day of their wedding, they give up their names for those of their husbands, and according to Morrison, everything is downhill from there. Rarely given opportunities to pursue their own interests, they become stilted and stunted versions of their former selves. Then, when their marriages fail, they collapse because they've been so wrapped up in the welfare of others for so many years that they no longer have identities of their own. But they can't collapse for long because now they have to do everything they were already doing plus what they depended on their husbands to do. To do anything less risks becoming a burden to the community and lowering their status in the social order.

This is the trap that Nel will fall into and Sula will manage to avoid, but each will pay a price. By placing the community's interests above her own, Nel won't have to develop any sense of self. The community will do that for her. Its values will enable her to see herself as a victim when Jude leaves her, encourage her to think of Sula as evil, and protect her from having to accept her corroborating role in the death of Chicken Little. Sula, on the other hand, will escape the degenerative influences of the community by placing herself at odds with its values, values she never had to think much about as a child because her unconventional family protected her from her neighbors' criticism. As an adult, she will be free to discover who she is in ways that are not open to Nel. But in turning her nose up at what the community thinks is important, Sula also turns her back on her own history and culture. Ironically, the cost of her independence is similar in many ways to the price Nel pays for her dependence: it stunts her intellectual and emotional growth. Because she has shrunk one level of awareness (her understanding of the norms of the community) to expand another (creating a lifestyle that meets her own needs), Sula will have sex with Nel's husband, be shocked to discover Nel's marriage means more to her than their friendship, and overlook her responsibility in Chicken Little's death. Nel and Sula may balance each other, but they do so from such extreme ends of the spectrum that they may not be as complementary as they first appear. To come to a better understanding of their relationship, let's take a closer look at Sula and Nel through the specific ways the conflict between community and self are presented and resolved in the novel. Let's start with Nel.

The only place in the black community where Nel is free to discover and explore who she is in her own right is in her relationship with Sula. When Nel is with Sula, she doesn't have to be concerned with what others may think of her. The freedom Nel enjoys with Sula, however, cannot equal the security she feels when she has won the approval of her husband, her family, and her community. Perhaps Sula knows this, and perhaps this is the reason why, when Nel peers into her husband's eyes for "one more look of reassurance" at the end of the wedding reception, she notices her friend heading toward the main road. The two "girls" will not see each other again for the next ten years.

Sula's return is foreshadowed by an omen in nature: all the robins die. There'll be no renewal this spring. Not in the black neighborhood of Medallion known as "the Bottom" anyway. Nel sees her excitement over the return of her friend reflected in water images: The month of May shimmers with evening showers and the afternoons are bright with the splashes of daffodils. Water, as we know from *The Bluest Eye*, is a traditional symbol of rebirth, and Nel tells us that getting Sula back will be like getting back the use of an eye after having a cataract removed. Her old life will be reborn; once again it will be interesting, imaginative, and magical. That she might have to take on additional responsibilities with Sula's arrival never enters Nel's head.

Four months after her return, Sula places her grandmother in Medallion's worst nursing home. It's run by the white church, and its inmates are mostly sick and poor. We know from *The Bluest Eye* what this means in a traditional black community. To be put out of your house by a fire or a landlord is catastrophic, but to be "put outdoors" by a member of your own family is unforgivable. There's no excuse for it. Sula's reason—that she simply wants control of the house—is such a serious violation of the community's code of behavior that she won't tell anybody. Nevertheless, she wants someone to support what she has done. So for the first time since Chicken Little drowned, Sula seeks her best friend's comfort, empathy, and approval.

But Nel is not the same Nel as she was ten years ago; she now shares the community's point of view and its values. She insists on knowing her friend's reason for putting Eva in a home. She gets two but doesn't buy either of them: not that Eva was sick and needed to be taken care of, and not that Eva was planning to kill Sula as she's rumored to have killed her only son almost a dozen years ago. When Sula's defensive tone becomes contrite—"I guess I should have stayed gone. I didn't know what else to do. Maybe I should have talked to you about it first. You always had better sense than me"—Nel responds the same way she does to her husband when he whines about how unfair his life is: She soothes the pain by making excuses. Never realizing that she's only encouraging the worst traits in the people she most loves, Nel rationalizes, "Sula, like always, was incapable of making any but the most trivial decisions. When it came to matters of grave importance, she behaved emotionally and irresponsibly and left it for others to straighten out."

Which is exactly what Nel does—just as she always has. Without wondering why it took Sula four months to get around to seeing her or why when she did come it was because she needed help and not necessarily to see how her best friend was faring, Nel agrees to go to the bank to have the money in Eva's account placed in Sula's name. She's about to set her mind to thinking of ways to make Eva more comfortable in the nursing home when Jude comes through the back door. As is his custom, he immediately launches into a tale of woe and self-pity that ends with his observation that black men have a hard row to hoe in this world.

But before Nel can rush to comfort her husband, Sula announces that the life of a black man looks pretty good to her. Jude's first response to this puzzling statement is anger at not being taken seriously, but Sula soon has both him and Nel laughing with a viewpoint they hadn't considered:

> White men love you. . . . The only thing they want to do is cut off a nigger's privates. And if that ain't love and respect, I don't know what is. And white women? They chase you all to every corner of the earth, feel for you under every bed. I knew a white woman wouldn't leave the house after 6 o'clock for fear one of you would snatch her. Now ain't that love? . . . Colored women worry themselves into bad health just trying to hang on to your cuffs. Even little children . . . spend all their childhood eating their hearts out 'cause they think you don't love them. And if that ain't enough, you love yourselves. . . . It looks to me like you the envy of the world.

And, one might add, someone Sula desires. In the next scene, she and Jude are naked on the floor of the Greenes' bedroom. Nel is in the doorway, and she can't believe what she is seeing. Jude gets up, puts on his pants, and walks out the door never to return, but all Nel can think of is that his fly is open and she doesn't want anyone to see him with his zipper down. And she won't say anything in front of Sula because she doesn't want to embarrass her husband.

Perhaps the worst part of this scene is the pain Nel feels when she sees Jude looking at her with the same disgust in his eyes as those of the soldiers who turned her mother into "custard" on the train to New Orleans. He's the one who cheated on her, yet she's the one who somehow betrayed him. How can this be? She's the one who placed Jude's fragile ego above her own, sacrificed the best part of her friendship with Sula to marry him, put on hold her own development as a human being to help build a family, made her personal needs secondary to what the community expected of her as a wife and mother, and what reward has she reaped in return? Seeing her husband and her best friend naked together on the bedroom floor.

Nel runs to the bathroom. On her knees, holding the rim of the tub, she waits for something dramatic to happen. What she'd once thought was unbecoming behavior— the shrieking and hand wringing she saw among the women at Chicken Little's funeral—now seems fitting to her. Good taste in the company of severe loss is not only inappropriate, it's unnatural. What's both natural and appropriate is to wave your arms, let your eyes roll, and scream your lungs out.

Nel does none of these things. As upset as she is, her only feeling is an internal movement that the narrator likens to the stirring of mud and dead leaves. Nel remembers Sula telling her that the real hell of hell is doing the same thing forever, but she now realizes her friend was wrong: the real hell of hell is change. And nothing after this day in hell will ever be the same for Nel. Then it hits her. Here she is at the lowest point of her life and what's she thinking of? Something Sula has said. She should be thinking about herself, but Nel hasn't done that in so long she's forgotten how. And what happened to that magnificent howl she went into the bathroom to release? Why doesn't it come? And what is this gray ball of fur and string and hair that appears in its place? It scares Nel so much she's afraid to look at it. She closes her eyes, sneaks past it, and shuts the door behind her, but it's still there. It follows her into the kitchen, out on the back porch, and everywhere she goes for the next twenty-eight years.

What do you think this fur ball symbolizes? Does it have something to do with Jude and Sula or is it something in herself that Nel is afraid to look at? Or does the fur ball symbolize the personal needs Nel has submerged so her husband can feel like a man? Could the ball be reminding Nel of what a coward she is because she's afraid to look at the person she's become after ten years of marriage? Or does it represent her inability to feel deeply? Because she can't feel the kind of pain that comes with serious loss, does that mean she can't feel deep love either? And if she can't love deeply, does that mean she never really loved Jude in the first place? If only Sula were there. She'd know how to make the fur ball go away. But Nel can't go to Sula because they're not talking since Jude walked out on her. So why does Nel go on thinking as if she and Sula are still best friends? And what does it mean when your husband leaves you for your best friend and she's the one you miss?

Morrison doesn't provide any answers for these questions. She wants us, as participating readers, to think about what's happened to Nel, Jude, and Sula and come up with our own ideas as to why these characters may be acting the ways they do. Morrison underscores her belief in multiple interpretations through a symbol in *Sula* that is most often mentioned in the chapter where Jude betrays Nel: Sula's birthmark. It means different things to different people depending on who's looking at it. The narrator describes the birthmark as a "stemmed rose" that spreads from the middle of Sula's eyelid to her eyebrow, but we're never told which eye. When Nel sees it for the first time in ten years, she notices that it gives Sula's glance "a suggestion of startled pleasure." But Nel's children see it as "a scary thing" that "leaps" when Sula talks, and in an obvious reference to Adam and Eve in the Garden of Eden, it reminds Jude of a snake. A poisonous one, of course, for this perpetual victim: a "copperhead" or a "rattler." Later in the story, one of the townspeople sees the birthmark as the ashes of Sula's mother who burned to death, others see it as a sign of "evil," and Shadrack, who lives by the river and is associated with water images throughout the novel, sees it as a "tadpole."

Sula, who has rebelled against conventionality since childhood, is surprised and saddened by Nel's response to her having sex with Jude. Hadn't they always compared how a boy kissed and what lines he used? Since when had Nel become so possessive? Hadn't they agreed that married women were never really jealous of other women but only afraid of losing their jobs as wives? Since when had Nel become "one of *them*"? If Sula had known Nel was going to react the way "others would have," she would not have seduced Jude. Nel was one of the reasons she'd drifted back to the Bottom. Now her best friend "belonged to the town and all its ways."

The narrator tells us that if Sula had "paints, or clay, or knew the discipline of the dance, or strings; had she anything to engage her tremendous curiosity and her gift for metaphor, she might have exchanged the restlessness and preoccupation with whim for an activity that provided her with all she yearned for." Restlessness? Preoccupation with whim? Are these what motivated Sula to make love with Jude? The narrator claims Sula has become dangerous because she's an artist with no art form. Art is supposed to enrich life by giving it meaning, but can any art form contain what it would have taken to provide Sula with "all she yearned for"? Many artists are seen as threats to their communities because they challenge the status quo through their media, and some people think the best art is always subversive. Do you think Sula could be her own work of art?

Or do you think perhaps Sula is too wrapped up in herself. Though her quest to know and grow is admirable, she often puts her needs and wants above those of others and never seems to think about the consequences. Like her mother, Sula doesn't hesitate to sleep with as many men as she pleases, but she's not pleased with many of the men she sleeps with. Sex, for Sula, is a celebration of her own power. In fact, it's all she's concerned with. She forgets the names of most of the men she has sex with before she's finished with them and can't wait for them to fall asleep or leave so she can enjoy "the postcoital privateness in which she met herself, welcomed herself, and joined herself in matchless harmony." Lovemaking, in this sense, is not really making love at all. It's making Sula. The narrator describes Sula's narcissism this way: "She lived out her days exploring her own thoughts and emotions giving them full reign, feeling no obligation to please anybody unless their pleasure pleased her."

The continual exception to Sula's self-absorption is Nel. Sula grants Nel all the freedom she assumes for herself. Unfortunately, Nel is more interested in security. When Sula sleeps with Jude, she shatters her friendship with Nel but not the illusion upon which her friend's life is based. Trusting her husband and her best friend may have proved to be a false hope, but Nel continues to believe as much in the domestic fiction endorsed by her community as Sula believes in her fiction of independence through unconventional behavior. The truth of both these fictions probably lies somewhere between the pain of Nel, who is abandoned by Jude and left with three children to raise, and the pleasures of Sula, whose disregard for the community's values turns her into an outcast. Sula and Nel may not be so much two halves of the same whole but two extremes going in almost completely opposite directions. Both roads lead to death: one physical and the other mental.

Three years after having had sex with Jude, Sula is undergoing a painful death. There's no one to care for her because in her short thirty years of life, she has alienated just about everybody in the Bottom. And her biggest offense wasn't putting her grandmother in a nursing home or breaking up her best friend's marriage; it was supposedly sleeping with white men. In the eyes of the black community, there is "nothing lower she could do, nothing filthier." Nel, meanwhile, has been obsessively devoting herself to her children at the expense of her own psychic needs. But Nel's love for her children has hardened. The narrator describes it as a "love that, like a pan of syrup kept too long on the stove, had cooked out, leaving only its odor and a hard, sweet sludge, impossible to scrape off."

Nel visits her dying friend not to gloat but to be charitable. At the same time, she's still carrying a lot of repressed anger over what happened between Sula and her husband. Their meeting doesn't start off well. Sula has also been angry and self-pitying. To fortify herself against Nel's visit, she recalls that the one time she tried to protect her friend by cutting off her own finger tip, she earned not Nel's gratitude but her disgust. But did that really happen? Is Sula, whose only conscious lie was about her reason for sending Eva to the nursing home, revising the past to suit her present purpose? Is she creating another fiction to believe as truth?

Sula's behavior on her deathbed is consistent with her

behavior for the past thirty years. When Nel tells her she needs help, Sula says she wants to stay right where she is. When Nel tells her there's no reason to be proud, Sula says she likes her own dirt. When Nel argues that Sula can't have it all, her former friend wants to know why not. When Nel accuses her of thinking and acting like a man, Sula compares Nel to a tree stump and herself to a redwood. When Nel says Sula has nothing to show for her independence, Sula says she's got her mind, "which means I got me." Does Nel remember her childhood promise to herself to be "Me"? If so, she gives no indication. She demands to know why Sula made love with Jude. When she hears that Jude served no greater purpose than to fill up some space in an afternoon, Nel accuses Sula of not loving her, of not considering her best friend's feelings. She also accuses Sula of taking Jude away from his wife and family, to which Sula replies that she didn't kill him, she just had sex with him. She also asks Nel, "If we were such good friends, how come you couldn't get over it?"

Nel has avoided this question for three years. Like the other members of the Bottom, it was easier to believe that she was the innocent victim and Sula the evil victimizer. The truth of Sula's statement now embarrasses and irritates Nel. Not nearly as self-(W)righteous as she's been acting, she starts to leave, but Sula isn't through with her.

> "How you know?" Sula asked.
> "Know what?" Nel still wouldn't look at her.
> "About who was good. How you know it was you?"
> "What you mean?"
> "I mean maybe it wasn't you. Maybe it was me."

These are Sula's last words in the novel. As she has done all her life, she challenges the community's definition of what is good and what is evil as it is embodied in Nel.

She also communicates with Nel the way they've communicated since childhood, namely, by sharing with her friend what she's learned from her life of questioning and exploring. It is this kind of imaginative activity, Sula seems to be saying, that makes life worth living. Had she an artistic context into which to channel and express what she's learned, Morrison seems to be saying, Sula would have become subversive without necessarily becoming self-destructive.

When Sula dies, almost her very first thought in the afterlife is of her best friend: "Well, I'll be damned," she thought, "it didn't even hurt. Wait'll I tell Nel." The first part of this passage, "I'll be damned," is obviously ironic, but what about the last part? Has Nel played a bigger role in Sula's life than her pride has allowed her to admit? What do you think that role could be? How do you think Nel might have influenced Sula's thinking and behavior?

Sula dies the way she lived most of her life: free, independent, and alone in the self-made prison of her own exploratory imagination. Nel, on the other hand, retreats into her dead life of conventional behavior for the next twenty-five years. It's not until she visits Sula's grandmother on another mission of mercy that she's confronted with the truth of her best friend's final words. Eva, who confuses Nel with Sula, wants to hear the truth about Chicken Little's death. The truth that Nel will never admit to anyone is that she felt good watching the boy drown. And the credit she gave herself for being calm when Sula was hysterical was not maturity but "the tranquility that follows a joyful stimulation." Nevertheless, the damage has been done. Eva, like her namesake in the Garden of Eden, has introduced another to the knowledge of good and evil.

The thought that she isn't as good as she's led herself and others to believe drives Nel quickly from the nursing home. Passing the cemetery where Sula is buried, the names on the tombstones of the Peace family call out to her like a chant or perhaps even a plea: "PEACE 1895–1921, PEACE 1890–1923, PEACE 1910–1940, PEACE 1892–1959. The tombstones make Nel realize other truths she's been unwilling to admit: she'll never be at peace as long as she continues to shield herself from the role she played in Chicken Little's death, and she'll never have peace with Sula as long as she judges her friend by the values of the community. Leaves stir, mud shifts, a soft ball of fur scatters in the wind, and Nel realizes that all the time she thought she was missing Jude she was really missing her best friend. "We was girls together," she says as if explaining something to a part of herself that's just beginning to understand.

The tears that refused to come when her husband left her now flow onto Nel's chest. "O Lord, Sula," she cried, "girl, girl, girlgirlgirl." The cry is "loud and long" because Nel is no longer using the false shield of conventional morality to protect herself from the truth; she's finally making things right without the "W." Abandoning the fiction of attachment to Jude, she is able to break free of the conventional definition of goodness. No longer preoccupied with the ideas of propriety that prevented her from discovering important truths about herself and Sula, she is now able, like her ancestors in the Garden of Eden, to become human. Her pain has "no bottom and . . . no top" because it knows no bounds, just never ending and always repeating "circles and circles of sorrow."

Helene Wright and Hannah Peace. Like Geraldine in *The Bluest Eye*, Helene Wright is a self-hating African American who tries to eliminate any blackness in her life, and just as Geraldine does, she imposes her false values on her only child. For the same reasons that Geraldine makes sure Junior's hair is always cut short to prevent any "wool" from developing, Helene keeps Nel's hair in braids and forces her to wear a clothespin on her nose when she sleeps at night. Both women are emotionally distanced from their husbands.

Helene is luckier than most women of her kind. Her husband Wiley—who isn't very wily—is a "seaman" who's "in port" only three days out of every sixteen. The narrator tells us that Wiley's long absences "were quite bearable for Helene Wright, especially when, after nine years of marriage, her daughter was born."

Did you notice that "Helene" rhymes with "Geraldine"? Do you think this could be a sign of how the two are so much alike? Do you think the fact that their names rhyme with "Pauline" might also be intentional? If you do, you're right on target. These women are all in the business of being "good," of conforming to the community's norm through counterproductive service to others.

Helene was born in a New Orleans brothel and rescued by her grandmother who, with the help of the Virgin Mary, eliminated any sign of funk in the child. When she grew into a "respectable" young woman, she married Wiley, who set her up in a materially well-off house in Medallion, Ohio. Their daughter, Nel, had Wiley's broad nose, generous lips, and dark skin. This made Helene happy for two reasons: her daughter was not as "pretty" as she was, and she now had a project to work on. Under Helene's supervision, without any help from the Virgin Mary, Nel became obedient, polite, and unimaginative.

Because there were no Catholics in the Bottom in 1921, Helene joined the most conservative black church. She kept her eyes forward when people arrived late for service, established the tradition of putting flowers on the altar, and introduced the practice of having banquets for returning war veterans. She also enjoyed manipulating her husband and daughter and falling asleep at night with the comforting thought of how far she'd come since she left New Orleans.

So it is with mixed emotions that Helene hears that the grandmother who rescued her from the brothel is dying. She doesn't want to return to the South—even for a visit—but she feels obligated. Putting her manner, her bearing, and her daughter on a train, Helene doesn't get past the Ohio state line before a conductor kicks her and Nel out of the "whites only" car.

And this is just the beginning. By the time they reach Alabama, there are no more "colored toilets"; Helene and Nel are forced to squat in the fields surrounding the train stations and wipe themselves with leaves. Ironically, Helene doesn't feel much less comfortable folding leaves than she does walking into her grandmother's house in New Orleans. And it's not the fact that she's arrived too late to see her grandmother alive that bothers her. What really seems to get on her nerves is the sweet smell of gardenias. That and the "painted canary" in the yellow dress who brought them. "This is your . . . grandmother, Nel," Helene reluctantly tells her daughter.

Helene's mother hugs Nel in an embrace that's tighter and stronger than the child would have expected from someone with such thin arms. "'Voir! 'Voir!" the woman tells her granddaughter and is gone. When Nel asks her mom what "voir" [look] means, Helene tells her, "I don't talk Creole. And neither do you." And neither, we might note, is Nel curious enough to seek somewhere else the meaning of her grandmother's important message.

Helene no sooner returns to her home in the Bottom section of Medallion, than she lights the fire, makes dinner, and begins dusting the furniture. She also tells an exhausted Nel that as long as she's sitting on the couch doing nothing, she could be putting her time to good use. "You could be pulling your nose," she tells her daughter.

Helene demonstrates some of the disadvantages that result from being brought up (W)right. Her concerns as a Christian are focused on flowers and banquets rather than people, she uses sex to manipulate her husband, and the ways she stifles her daughter's development would be immoral if she had a clue as to the damage she was causing. Fortunately for Nel, she sees—if only temporarily—the "custard" that her mother's sense of propriety tries to mask.

And what is the custard that Helene tries to hide behind a starched husband, a submissive daughter, and a spotless house? Fear. She's afraid of the passion that might lie within herself when she makes love with Wiley, she's afraid of her mom's funk surfacing in Nel's behavior, and she's so afraid of the dirt and chaos she associates with black people that she starts dusting her house almost as soon as she steps off the train from New Orleans. Controlling her fear by manipulating people and objects into appearances that she perceives as socially acceptable, Helene never thinks about where her fear is coming from. It's easier and more rewarding to earn the approval of the community by helping others conform to its values.

When we meet Hannah Peace, her husband Rekus is dead and their daughter Sula is three years old. Hannah is a totally self-indulgent woman who operates almost completely outside the norms of socially acceptable behavior. Like her mother Eva, with whom she and Sula live, Hannah loves all men. And all men seem to love Hannah's easygoing, natural funk. She doesn't wear make-up, restrain her hair, wear shoes in the summer, or cover her feet in the winter in anything more glamorous than leather slippers with the backs flattened under the heels. Nevertheless, Hannah "rippled with sex . . . she made men aware of her behind, her slim ankles, the dew-smooth skin and the incredible length of neck."

Because she sees sex as an ordinary part of her life, Hannah refuses to live without the attention of men for so long as a single day. Most of her lovers are friends and neighbors, and she's known in the community to have broken up a few marriages, but no one thinks of her as "evil." The narrator describes her flirting as "sweet" and "guileless," and her lovemaking as "welcoming, light and playful." The men defend her against their wives and newcomers to the community.

What separates Hannah from so many of the other women in the Bottom is her attitude: She makes the many husbands she has sex with feel as if they don't "need fixing." That anyone could be complete and wonderful as they are is not only unexpected, it's unheard of. Nevertheless, Hannah draws the line at going to sleep with them; she's not willing to make the commitment that, in her mind, this level of intimacy requires. What Sula learns from her mother's behavior is that sex is frequently pleasant and pleasantly frequent "but otherwise unremarkable." Friendships like one she has with Nel are remarkable.

It is while developing her friendship with Nel that twelve-year-old Sula overhears her mother talking about the problems of child rearing with two of her women friends. When one of the women says she doesn't know if "love" is the word she'd used to describe how she feels about her daughter, Hannah tells her, "You love her, like I love Sula. I just don't like her." This pronouncement leads Sula to logically but mistakenly conclude that if her mother doesn't love her, she can't depend on her, and if she can't depend on her mother, she can't depend on anyone else either.

What's odd about these three generations of women is that for all their lovemaking with men, they don't seem to have an easy time connecting emotionally with each other. Although indifferent to social conventions, true to themselves, and honest when they speak with each other, the three women can't seem to combine their attitude toward what's wrong with society with the kind of love that would compensate for many of its deficiencies. Sula hears her mother say she doesn't like her, but she doesn't ask Hannah what she means by her statement. Hannah also isn't sure if her own mother loves her, but she does ask Eva, "Mamma, did you ever love us?"

The matriarch is furious. "You settin' here with your healthy-ass self and ax me did I love you? Them big old eyes in your head would have been two holes full of maggots if I hadn't." Hannah then makes matters worse by asking Eva, "Did you ever, you know, play with us." Eva tells her daughter that in 1895 nobody was "playin'," that "niggers were dying like flies," and that she sat in a house with her and her two siblings and three beets for five days: "What you talkin' 'bout did I love you girl I stayed alive for you can't you get that through your thick head or what is that between your ears, heifer?" Hannah, thanks to Eva, has never had to make sacrifices for Sula. Almost a perpetual child, she can't fully appreciate the behavior through which her mother expresses her love. As a result, Hannah may be sexually free, but she can't commit to others the way Eva has. She sees her daughter as a burden but doesn't think to sacrifice anything of herself to improve the condition of their relationship. In fact, she doesn't seem to do anything for Sula at any point in the entire novel. Certainly not the way Eva does. Having had everything done for her all her life it's easier for Hannah to just sit back and complain or let Eva do for the child what she doesn't have enough love to do herself.

Several days after their conversation, Eva shows Hannah just how much she loves her when, from her upstairs bedroom window, she sees her daughter's dress go up in flames as she's tending a fire in the front yard. Because there's no time to hobble down the stairs on her one leg, Eva breaks the bedroom window with her elbow and leaps to the rescue. Unfortunately, she lands short of the flames consuming her daughter, who runs down the street in a desperate search for someone to put out the fire. Both women are taken to the hospital, but Hannah dies on the way. "Or so they said," the narrator adds. Is this statement an indication of the treatment Hannah received at the hospital because she is black, or is it a hint from the narrator that Eva may have killed her daughter in the ambulance to put her out of the misery that would last the rest of her life? Because nobody's talking, we have to figure out for ourselves what we think might have happened. Whichever way you choose contributes to the story. Not being able to choose also contributes. What's important is to consider the possibilities.

Eva is shaken by her daughter's sudden and painful death, but what she can't get out of her mind is an equally disturbing image of Sula. While Eva was trying to drag herself along the ground in her vain attempt to save Hannah, she noticed Sula was standing on the back porch watching her mother burn. And she wasn't "paralyzed" by the horror taking place before her eyes; she was "interested."

Water closing over Chicken Little, her mother going up in flames, even her own death Sula is able to see from a curious, disinterested perspective. Nevertheless, the last image we have of her is not without emotion. She's on her deathbed awash in pain with her legs drawn up to her chest. Her eyes closed, her thumb in her mouth, she waits in weary anticipation "until she met a rain scent and would know the water was near, and she would curl into its heavy softness and it would envelop her, carry her, and wash her tired flesh always." Like Hannah and like Cholly Breedlove curling up by the waters of the Ocmulgee River in *The Bluest Eye*, Sula yearns for the maternal, womblike nurturing she doesn't believe she's ever received.

Rochelle Sabat and Eva Peace. Rochelle, who is Helene's mother and Nel's grandmother, doesn't stay around for long in *Sula*, but her splash ripples throughout the novel. A "Creole whore," Rochelle gave birth to Helene behind the red shutters of the Sundown House in New Orleans. Rochelle's mother Cecile "rescued" Helene from the soft lights and flowered carpets of the brothel and, with the help of the Virgin Mary, guarded her against any signs of her daughter's wild blood for the next sixteen years. And how about the name "Sabat"? Sabats are secret places where witches rendezvous. No chance of Helene showing up at one of these. Under Cecile's wing, her name could just as well be "Sabbath," a day of religious observance among Jews and Christians. We meet Rochelle in November of 1920. Cecile has died, and Helene and Nel have arrived too late. Three statues of the Virgin Mary protect the front room, but they can't prevent ten-year-old Nel from being impressed with her forty-eight-year-old grandmother. In contrast to the "sigh of death" in every corner of every room, Rochelle wears a loud, convention-ally inappropriate yellow dress, smells of gardenias, and darkens her eyebrows with the heads of burnt match-sticks. This symbol of life in a house of death leans forward to embrace her granddaughter, but Helene interferes. "We have to get cleaned up," she insists. "We been three days on the train with no chance to wash or . . ."

Rochelle gets the message, starts to leave, then sud-denly squeezes her granddaughter in a hug that is more powerful than Nel would have thought possible. "She smelled so nice," Nel later tells her mother while Helene soaps off any residue Rochelle might have left on the child, "and her skin was so soft." "Much handled things are always soft," Helene replies in an obvious attempt to turn her daughter against her grandmother.

Rochelle stands in opposition to and subverts the val-ues of "good" women like Helene. Her illegal job, her immoral behavior, her gaudy clothes, her unrestrained laughter, her marital status, her "illegitimate" child, her insistence on speaking French, and the hair she wears in "halo-like rolls" all signify her refusal to abide by the codes of respectable, middle-class conventionality. So does her spontaneous and deeply felt affection for Nel.

Rochelle may sell her body, but she hasn't, like Helene, prostituted herself for material comforts and social acceptability.

Nel is excited by Rochelle. And the grandmother's brief but penetrating influence on the child can't be washed away. No wonder Nel is so eager to be friends with Sula when she returns from New Orleans. Sula is the closest thing to Rochelle in all of Medallion.

There are few characters in American literature who can compare with Eva Peace. A life-giving, almost mythical God the Mother, she can also kill. Our first view of Eva is of her directing the lives of her children, friends, strays, and a stream of boarders from the top floor of her three-story boarding house at 7 Carpenter's Road. This address, with its possible allusion to the sacrificing carpenter Jesus or perhaps a reference to God the Father's constructing the world in seven days, is no coincidence. Eva's heavenly throne is a rocking chair propped on top of a child's wagon that enables her to move about more easily since she lost one of her legs. People look down when they talk to her, but they feel as if they are looking up.

How Eva lost her leg also borders on myth. Children hear stories that range from the leg getting up by itself and walking off before Eva could catch it to a corn eating the leg up to Eva's knee before she could stop it with a red rag. Adults speculate that Eva stuck her leg under a train to collect the insurance money that enabled her to build her house and support her three children. Or perhaps she sold it to a hospital for $10,000.

However she sacrificed it, Eva isn't saying. She also flaunts her missing leg by showing off the other one in calf-length skirts and fancy shoes. Obviously it's an important symbol for her, the black community, and Morrison. What do you think the missing leg could stand for? How about the lack of understanding and empathy among the women in the Peace household? Or a society that, because it allows men to abandon their families without having to be responsible for those they leave behind, often forces single mothers to take desperate steps to ensure their children's survival?

Eva was once married to a man called "BoyBoy." That his name is redundant indicates just how much of a child he was. After five years of getting drunk, abusing Eva, and screwing around with other women, BoyBoy abandoned his wife, their eldest daughter Hannah, a middle child called "Pearl," and a son known as "Plum." Eva was left with three kids, five eggs, three beets, $1.65, and an approaching winter. The neighbors helped out, but they weren't much better off than Eva. Hannah was too young to care for her sister and brother, and any housework Eva could find would keep her away from her children from before five in the morning until after eight at night. But she wouldn't return to her family in Virginia; that particular humiliation would be worse than losing a limb.

By December, Plum stopped having bowel movements. Eva took her son to the outhouse, stuck her finger up his anus, snagged what felt like a pebble, freed the blockage, and returned to her bed to think. Two days later, she left her three children with a neighbor, saying she would be back the next day. That day lasted eighteen months. Sweeping down from a wagon with two crutches, a new pocketbook, and one leg, Eva gave her neighbor a ten-dollar bill and started building the boardinghouse on Carpenter's Road.

Thus begins the myth of a new kind of Eve. Neither the traditional wife of a conventional Adam in a "respectable" Garden of Medallion nor an abandoned victim whose family is a burden to the community, this Eva—like the Christian god in heaven who sacrificed his son for the salvation of humankind—sacrificed her leg for the salvation of her children. Now the missing leg also symbolizes pride and defiance. Eva is not going to give anyone an opportunity to either gloat or pity her, and she is going to show the members of her community that she can not only survive with her children, she can triumph over the economic conditions that forced her to behave so radically.

BoyBoy also returns to the Bottom, but he shows up with a woman who laughs like she's spent some time in a big city. The laughter hits Eva with all the subtlety of a sledgehammer, and she knows the subsequent hate that fills her heart will protect and strengthen her for as long as she needs it. When Hannah accuses her of hating black people, Eva says she only hates one, and hating him is what keeps her alive and happy. Do you think the missing leg possibly represents Eva's hatred of BoyBoy since he's the one who left her without a leg to stand on?

Among Eva's boarders is a white man who wants to drink himself to death in peace, and Landlady Peace is happy to oblige him. People called the man "Pretty Johnnie" when he first moved in and said he was half white, but Eva dubbed him "Tar Baby" as a mean sort of joke, and the name stuck. She also houses three homeless boys. One is white, one is black, and one is Mexican. Although their ages were seven, five, and four by the time Sula was eleven, and they all arrived independently of one another, Eva called each of the boys "Dewey" and put them all in the same class at school. Their names, like "BoyBoy," are redundant, and their behavior reminds some readers of Donald Duck's three nephews. That the three "Deweys"—they're all under five feet tall—become "deweys" with a small "d" underscores Morrison's belief that when you name a person, place, or thing, you can control in a significant way the behavior or fate of that person, place, or thing. No one knows Tar Baby's real name or any longer thinks of him as "pretty"; the deweys cannot be individually identified; and BoyBoy never acts like an adult.

95

But "naming" doesn't always work the way it's supposed to. Eva called her second child "Pearl," but she turned out to be more like sand in the Peace oyster. She married at fourteen, moved to Michigan, and for years sent her mother dull letters with two dollar bills folded into the writing paper. Nor did Eva's drug-addicted son turn out to be much of a "Plum."

Eva believes in the traditional values of love and family. She advises the newlywed women who board at her house to make proper meals for their husbands and be sure their clothes are clean and well pressed. At the same time, Eva does not believe conventional codes of behavior should interfere in the ways people act—a philosophy she passes on to her offspring. Hannah, who moves in with Eva when her husband dies and Sula is three, has as many male lovers as her mother has "gentleman callers."

Eva and Hannah pass on to Sula their free-wielding senses of spirit and independence, as well as an attitude that isn't much affected by criticism. But for all their freedom of expression and relations with men, there doesn't seem to be much affection or understanding of each other among the three women. Eva repeats her stories of sacrifice without realizing that, though they may contain the pain, anger, and love of her experience as a matriarch, they are just stories to Hannah and Sula because they haven't lived through them. They don't realize that in order to survive and provide, Eva may have had to separate herself from her children in the emotional ways that have become important to her daughter and granddaughter. In other words, Eva's words about her sacrifices don't say, "I love you" the way her Hannah and Sula need to feel it.

"What about Plum?" Hannah asks Eva in a final attempt to know if her mother really loved her children. How can she love her drug-addicted son if she killed him? Eva tells her daughter that Plum was regressing. She says he wanted to crawl back into her womb and there wasn't any room. Room in her heart, yes, but in her womb, no. "Thinking baby thoughts and dreaming baby dreams and messing up his pants again and smiling all the time," Plum was stoned out of his mind. He was on his way to becoming the Bottom's oldest living infant. That's why Eva killed him. She wanted him to die while he was still a man. Or at least looked like one. "I did everything I could to make him leave me and go on and live and be a man," she tells Hannah, "but he wouldn't and I had to keep him out so I just thought of a way he could die like a man, not all scrunched up inside my womb, but a man."

What about Plum? With the exception of BoyBoy, the one thing all three Peace women have in common is their love of men. Perhaps her love of maleness is the reason Eva was so partial to her son, who "floated in a constant swaddle of love and affection" until he went off to war in 1917. He was back in the Bottom by 1920, but he'd been changed by the war. He stole money from the women, made frequent trips to Cincinnati, and slept for days in his room with the record player going. After Hannah found the spoon burned black from heroin, Eva decided to act: she set her only son on fire while he lay in a drugged stupor in his bed. "But I held him close first," she later tells her daughter through a veil of tears. "Real close. Sweet Plum. My baby boy."

At least one critic, Roberta Rubenstein, believes that Eva's emotionally charged defense of her murdering Plum is really a disguised incest wish. Eva wants to make love with her son and fears the impulse within her that might allow her to do it. Listen to the way she describes her perception that Plum is trying to get into her womb: "When I closed my eyes I'd see him . . . and he'd be creepin' to the bed trying to spread my legs trying to get back up in my womb. . . . I kept on dreaming it. . . . One night it wouldn't be no dream. It'd be true and I would have done it, would have let him if I'd've had the room. . . ." Rubenstein claims that Eva's eloquence almost makes you believe that the idea to enter her is Plum's wish and not her own. Could this be true? And if it were, how does that affect your perception of Eva's murder? Eva would like us to think that what she's done is a sacrifice on her part. She'd like us to think she killed Plum to save him from becoming a vegetable. And even if her sacrifice is justified in her mind, does that give Eva the right to take Plum's life?

Although Hannah and Sula have not learned to appreciate fully the sacrifices Eva has made on their behalf, they have learned her lessons of arrogance and power. Hannah leads an almost totally self-absorbed, self-defined life, while Sula allows Chicken Little to drown, watches Hannah burn to death, and throws Eva into a nursing home without a moment's hesitation. Unlike her mother, however, Sula is willing to sacrifice. In a misguided attempt to echo her grandmother's cutting off her leg for the survival of the Peace family, Sula cuts off the tip of her finger to protect Nel from the Irish hoodlums.

Fourteen years after Hannah's death, Sula returns to the Bottom in 1937. No one has seen or heard from her in the ten years since she walked out of Nel's wedding reception. Eva looks at her granddaughter the same way she looked at BoyBoy when he returned in 1921. "When you gone to get married?" she asks. "You need to have some babies. It'll settle you." Sula tells Eva she has a mind to do to her what she did to Plum. Eva never goes to sleep without locking her door from that moment on, but it doesn't stop Sula from getting rid of her. Within four months, the proud matriarch is carted off to the worst nursing home in Medallion.

Forty-four years after Plum's death in 1921, forty-years after Hannah's death in 1923, and twenty-five years after Sula's death in 1940, Nel visits Eva in her room at the nursing home. The year is 1965. Eva, who's obviously been around a long time, still has a few questions she'd like answered. Confusing Nel with Sula, she insists on knowing the truth about Chicken Little's death.

Unable to hide behind her mission of mercy or satisfy Eva's curiosity with anything less than the truth, Nel flees the nursing home. She admits to herself what she's never told anybody: she was excited watching the boy drown, and she convinced Sula there was no need to report what happened because nothing would bring Chicken Little back to life. Accepting the fact that she is not as "good" as she has led herself and others to believe allows Nel to look at who she is rather than how she has tried to appear all her life. She realizes that her adherence to conventional standards of morality and respectability have prevented her from knowing who she is as a person, deprived her of a unique and valuable friend, and kept her from developing as an independent human being. Still, it's not too late. Because of the Mother Goddess's insistence on truth, Nel is able to appreciate the message of Sula, mourn the loss of her friend, and renew the process of becoming the "Me" she promised herself she would be when she was ten years old.

Jude Greene. Jude is twenty, handsome, well-liked, and respectable. A tenor in the church quartet, he could have had his pick of eight or ten young women, but he chose seventeen-year-old Nel, the only woman he knew who didn't seem hell-bent on marrying. The odd thing is that Jude wasn't all that keen on marriage either until he failed to get a job building the new road and tunnel that would link his town with towns on the other side of the river.

A waiter at the Hotel Medallion, Jude sees construction work as an opportunity to dirty his hands with something other than potato peelings. He wants to wear work shoes, swing a pick, shovel gravel, and enjoy the camaraderie of men who earn their living by using their muscles.

He wants to produce something he can point to and say, "I built that road." It was while filling his head with dreams about sledgehammers, pickaxes, lunch buckets, and work clothes that he talked with Nel about getting married. She was open to but not terribly excited by the idea.

When Jude saw smaller and skinnier white boys getting the construction jobs he knew he could do faster and better, he got the same message sent to black men all over the country for hundreds of years. And the message hurt. That's when he started pressing Nel to be his wife. If he couldn't be a man on the road he'd be one in a home of his own making. Married to Nel he wouldn't just be a waiter hanging around a kitchen like a powerless woman; he would be the head of a family working in a hotel because he had no other choice. The more he thought about the idea, the more attractive it became. Nel would heal his hurt, soothe his pain, and care for him like a mother, only not like his mother because his mother would always see him as her boy no matter how old he was or what work he did. Nel would do what his mother couldn't, namely, provide him with a role that would enable him to be seen as a man. He in return would love Nel, provide for her, and protect her from harm. "The two of them together," the narrator informs us, "would make one Jude."

Like most women who see themselves from the perspective of others, Nel was flattered by Jude's attention. She had always thought that her smile was a parting of her lips until she saw in Jude's eyes that it was a miracle. Sula didn't care much about her friend's neck or smile and, according to the narrator, appreciated the attention Jude showered on Nel almost as much as Nel did. In Sula's mind, Jude's compliments to Nel were as much compliments to herself as the cruelty of the Irish boys years earlier was a challenge. What Nel found especially meaningful in Jude that she didn't experience with Sula, however, was this: Jude made Nel feel needed.

So if Jude successfully exploits Nel's willingness to care for him as his mother does, and Nel willingly sacrifices her development as a human being to serve Jude's pursuit of his masculine ego, what's the problem? Why do you think Jude feels the need to make love with Sula? The most likely answer is because she was there, she had some time to fill, and she felt like it. Jude probably had very little to do with what happened. He may have enjoyed a brief moment of physical pleasure and had his delicate image of himself momentarily massaged, but he didn't get anything else from Sula, whose narcissistic building of her own ego would eclipse any other interest she might have had in him. And as she has done with every other man in her life up to this point, Sula liked Jude, laid Jude, and left Jude.

Jude leaves his home and family after betraying them for Sula, but he doesn't suffer the psychic disintegration that Nel does because his manhood has been enhanced by his infidelity. This, after all, is what "men" do. It's one of the things that makes them "men." Jude's wife, on the other hand, withers because her identity has been tied up for so long with her husband's enormous but fragile ego. But she can't stay depressed for long because she has three kids and the people in her community expect her to be responsible in all the ways they know most men aren't. It is in this demoralized state that Nel wraps herself in the cloak of martyrdom and joins the ranks of all the other women in the Bottom whose husbands got going when the going got tough. She also uses the community's sense of responsibility to her children to protect herself as the wronged wife from the truth that the real loss in her life was not Jude; it was Sula.

Albert Jacks. Flight is also on the mind of Albert Jacks. He loves airplanes and makes frequent trips to Dayton where there is a military airbase as well as an airport. He even goes by an adventuresome name with mythic roots: "Ajax." But Ajax's flights are more flights of fantasy than anything else; he has no more of a chance of sitting at the controls of an airplane in a racist culture than Jude has of working in the construction industry. And for all his high-altitude dreams, none of them include any mention of that dreaded "r" word so many of the black men in Morrison's novels are flying away from: "responsibility."

"Ajax" is the name of an ancient Greek hero who distinguished himself in the Trojan War by rescuing the body of Achilles. He then killed himself when Odysseus was given Achilles' armor instead of him.

Ajax doesn't have a wife or a family or a job, but he is willing to take care of himself. The narrator describes Ajax as a "pool haunt of sinister beauty." With no wife and no job, he is free in the irresponsible ways that Morrison finds so attractive in some men. He is also endearingly unconventional—especially to Sula. If he wants to pick up a present for someone, he's not above stealing it from a white family. He may be the only person in the novel not to try to turn her birthmark into a symbol, and he is the only one capable of having a "genuine conversation" with her. And unlike Jude, Ajax hasn't allowed his ego to be diminished by racism. Nor does he need a wife to mother him.

When Ajax and Sula get together, they are not two halves trying to make an Ajax or even construct two parts of themselves into a whole. They are independent, self-sufficient, self-contained human beings who want to be with each other for no other reason than that they enjoy each other's company. There are no restrictions and no demands. That is until Sula, in a rare moment of conventionality, cleans her house, takes a bath, sets the table, and puts a green ribbon in her hair.

Ajax has seen this kind of behavior before and he knows exactly what's going to come next: a talk about settling down, getting a job, and starting a family. When he sees these signs of domesticity, "every hackle" on Ajax's body rises, and his eyes dim with a "mild and momentary regret." He also knows what he needs to do before he gets saddled with a wife and kids: FLY! It is important to note, however, that Ajax's taking off from Sula at the first signs of her uncharacteristic possessiveness is not a betrayal like Jude's running away from Nel. Ajax's flight is a soaring exercise in self-preservation.

But there may be another reason why Ajax heads into the wild blue yonder above the tarmac in Dayton. His mother. He may not be able to love another woman. A well-traveled voyager on the road of the occult, she raised him without demands, encouraged him to answer only to his own whims, taught him to cherish his freedom, and reminded him to always be kind to others.

Ajax loved his mother, "and after her—airplanes. There was nothing in between." His initial attraction to Sula is that her indifference to established norms of behavior reminds him of his mother. He suspects that Sula may be the only other woman whose life is really her own. Sula is someone "who could deal with life efficiently, and who was not interested in nailing him." But she is. When Sula tells Ajax, "Come on. Lean on me," she sounds just like Nel. How much like Nel she is comes to the surface after Ajax flies from her nest: She discovers from the driver's license he left behind that his name isn't "Ajax" but "Albert Jacks." A. Jacks. Presented this way, it looks more like a kid's game than the name of an ancient Greek hero. Sula concludes the whole experience with Ajax was little more than a fantasy: "I didn't even know his name. And if I didn't know his name, then there is nothing I did know and I have known nothing ever at all since the one thing I wanted was to know his name so how could he help but leave me since he was making love to a woman who didn't even know his name."

Sula didn't know his game either. The kind of love that is

accompanied by deep feelings for anyone but his mother threatens Ajax's sense of independence; it also thwarts Sula's quest for self-development. If Ajax had been a little more like Nel, he might have seen in Sula the aloneness, which is different than loneliness, that often results when a woman is rejected by her community for acting like a man. But because he is more like Sula, who is incapable of empathy, Ajax can't see past his own immediate and somewhat childish needs. Airplanes. Of all things. Ajax is not the partner or friend Sula gave him credit for being. Shadrack who, like Sula, is also an outcast of the community, may be more likely to understand how she feels. Do you think this may be the reason he is the last man she thinks of before dying? Or do you think Sula's unexpected, uncharacteristic, unexplained desire to "possess" Ajax might be the result of something as simple as the seductive power of a conventional romantic plot? Or could it be that Morrison wants us to see that no one is entirely free of conventional influences? What other reason can you think of for Sula to have acted the way she did?

And what is it with these men and their mothers? Plum wants to crawl back into the safety and comfort of Eva's womb, Jude wants a wife who will mother him but make him feel like a man instead of a boy, and Ajax is only attracted to women who remind him of his mother. Where do the women of the Bottom go to find husbands when all the men still belong to their mothers?

The Peace women also yearn for mother-love. Hannah wants Eva to tell her she loves her—and Eva can't or won't say the words—and Sula assumes the license to kill Chicken Little and watch her mother die when she hears Hannah "loves" her but doesn't "like" her. When she dies, Sula is curled up in a fetal position with her thumb in her mouth. Could all this talk about freedom and independence and self-development and unconventional behavior be the result of unresolved Oedipal fixations in a few adults who've never been able to grow up?

Shadrack. Shadrack is one of many veterans "blasted and permanently astonished" by his experiences in World War I. At the time this psychological condition was called "shell shock"; today it's known as "post-traumatic stress disorder." Not yet twenty years of age, Shadrack was running across a battlefield in France when he turned to see the head of one of his comrades fly off: "But . . . the body of the headless soldier ran on, with energy and grace, ignoring altogether the drip and slide of brain tissue down its back."

This would send into a straitjacket many people unprepared and unable to register such a sight. Shadrack is no exception. He winds up in a veteran's hospital where his hands grow like Jack's beanstalk whenever they appear from beneath his bedcovers, and the staff always refers to him as "Private," as in "We're not going to have any trouble today, are we? Are we, Private?" At least they have the courtesy to call him by his rank. Most of the black soldiers returning from Europe in 1917 expected to be treated as heroes and rewarded for the sacrifices they had made for their country; instead they were reduced to the same social and economic status they held before the war.

Because there are more soldiers in need of treatment than there is available space, Shadrack is prematurely released from the hospital with "no past, no language, no tribe, no source, no address book, no comb, no pencil, no clock, no pocket handkerchief, no rug . . . no tobacco pouch, no soiled underwear and nothing nothing nothing to do." The bullet that shattered his comrade's brain has also shattered Shadrack's mind. It's left him with no sense of identity. There is nothing in his life to indicate who he might be. Without a home, family, or community, he is lost in a world that has no order and, like himself, no name. Only "Private," which Shadrack associates not with his military rank but a secret. Why, he often wonders, do people call him a secret?

Unable to function without an identity in a world without an order that makes sense to him, Shadrack winds up in jail on charges of intoxication and vagrancy. During the night he sees his reflection in the water of the toilet in his cell. The image astonishes him. He'd been thinking he was not real—that he really didn't exist—but now he sees that he's a black man. The fact that he recognizes himself as a human being enables Shadrack to sleep deeper than he has for more than a year.

When he is released from jail, Shadrack discovers his hospital bed and the window from which he dreamed of a river full of fish are only twenty miles from his hometown of Medallion. The next twelve days are a struggle to order and focus his experience in the war. Not so much the death part, but the sudden unexpectedness of death. That's what really frightens Shadrack. His solution is to create an annual parade during which all the people in the community can get their fear of unexpected death out of their systems until the same day the following year. The ritual becomes known as "National Suicide Day."

Every January 3 starting in 1920, Shadrack marches through the Bottom with a hangman's rope and a cowbell. This is the people's only chance each year to kill themselves or each other. At first the people of Bottom think this Shadrack who lives in a riverbank cabin once owned by his grandfather is crazy, but that doesn't mean he has no sense or, more importantly, no power. Who else among them could curse white people and get away with it? Eventually Shadrack and National Suicide Day become woven into the fabric of the community. A woman may note, for example, that her labor pains started on Suicide Day, or a farmer might comment that one of his chickens started laying double-yolk eggs right after Suicide Day.

By creating a ritual to symbolically heal himself and control his fear of unexpected death, Shadrack shows that he can be responsible for his own well-being; by inviting others to participate in his parade, he also demonstrates that he is concerned about the well-being of the community. The rebirth symbolized by the water in the toilet is now complete and symbolically confirmed by the river Shadrack fishes from to earn his living.

Compare for a moment Shadrack's response to his experiences in World War I with those of Eva's son Plum. By turning his fear of unexpected death into a creative act that involves the community, Shadrack determines the direction of his life. His craziness may make him an outsider, but he is not a pariah like Sula, whom the community thinks is evil. Plum, on the other hand, wanders around the country for a year after the war and shows up in Medallion with "a black bag, a paper sack, and a sweet, sweet smile." He closets himself in his room and falls deeper and deeper under the influence of drugs.

In the bible story, Shadrack is one of the people in the burning furnace with Daniel. Like his biblical namesake who survives the fiery furnace, Shadrack survives the fire of World War I, while Plum goes up in the flames set by his mother. Water is used as a symbol of rebirth in both *The Bluest Eye* and *Sula*, but fire can also symbolize a new beginning. Representing fire this way comes from a myth created in the ancient civilization of Phoenicia, a country that existed where Syria, Lebanon, and Israel are today. The story is of a beautiful bird known as a "Phoenix" that could live up to 500 or 600 years. The bird would burn itself to death, then rise in youth from its own ashes to live another long life. Shadrack is reborn into a new life from the ashes of World War I; Plum is also reborn from his fiery death, but only if you believe he sends messages to Eva in the nursing home. Eva claims she has been talking to Plum when she wants Nel to tell her the truth about the role she and Sula played in Chicken Little's drowning. If, however, you think Eva is making up her story about talking with Plum to pressure Nel into telling the truth, then her son's death by fire is not a rebirth. He's nothing but ashes.

Shadrack says only one word in the whole novel. He says it when Sula runs into his cabin to see if he saw her and Nel watch Chicken Little drown instead of rescuing him. The word is "Always." This is a strange word to say to a child standing in the middle of your living room. Especially one you've just seen throw an innocent boy into a river and watch him die. What do you think Shadrack means? The narrator tells us Shadrack tells Sula "always" because he wants her to believe that she is permanent and doesn't have to worry about dying like Chicken Little did. Critics who believe this is the reason support their interpretation by pointing out that just before he says these words, Shadrack is looking at the skull that exists under the skin of Sula's face. These same critics confirm their view by telling us that when Shadrack sees Sula dead in the funeral home, he realizes that there is no "always" and that he cannot control death by naming a day and instituting a parade.

Other critics disagree. They claim the word "always" refers not to death but change, and Shadrack is assuring Sula that nothing will change because of Chicken Little's death. Unfortunately for Sula, this is true. She's the same selfish, stubborn person on her deathbed as she was on the day Chicken Little died. Still other critics say Shadrack is referring to personal convictions. He's telling Sula that, like him, she always has to be true to what she believes in. Still other critics claim Shadrack is talking about the emotions surrounding the death of the little boy. These emotions will "always" be with Sula no matter what she does or how long she lives. And just when you think there can't possibly be another interpretation, some critics claim Shadrack is talking about how the fear of unexpected death will never go away because unexpected death can never be prevented. This interpretation is supported by the fact that so many people from the community unexpectedly die in the National Suicide Day parade that takes place in 1941. So which is it? (A) All of the above. (B) None of the above. (C) Some of the above. (D) More than the above.

The Community. The town where the action in *Sula* takes place is called "Medallion," but the black community is known as "the Bottom." The name "Bottom" is a comment about how black people have to endure so much that is upside down for them, but there's also a story behind the naming. At some point in the first half of the nineteenth century, a white farmer promised one of his slaves his freedom and "a piece of bottom land" if the man would complete a difficult task. When the slave finished his work, the farmer had second thoughts about the land part of his promise. So instead of giving his former slave a portion of the fertile valley, he set aside a tract up in the hills, where the good soil had been eroded and the constant wind prevented much from growing.

The freed man questioned why he wasn't being given land in the area he had been promised, and the farmer claimed he was getting a better deal than the one they had agreed to. Yes, the land was in the hills, but when God looked down it was the "bottom of heaven." That's why it was called "the Bottom"; it was "the best land there is." Now the freed man knew bad land when he saw it, but what choice did he have? There was no written contract, and even if there were, the people determining his fate would all be white.

The black people who come to live in the Bottom see this story of their community as representative of the dishonesty inherent in white people's logic, the manipulation apparent in the way they use language, and the injustice contained in the laws they write to protect themselves. White people, of course, interpret the story as a testament to their own savvy and the gullibility of black people. Both groups laugh about the story but each laughs for a different reason.

Ironically, the land on the "Bottom" comes out on top when the black people who live there manage to turn it into a neighborhood where just about everybody but Sula and Hannah know, care about, and are willing to support each other. There's music, laughter, stories, fun, and some pretty amazing characters. In the valley, which has come to represent commerce, business, and industry, the people have traded the qualities that made them interesting as human beings for the material goods money can by. Compare Eva, Hannah, Sula, Nel, Jude, Ajax, and others with those white people who've been dehumanized by the false values they live by in Medallion: there's the farmer who cheats his slave out of the land he earned, the police officer who arrests mentally disturbed Shadrack for drunkenness and vagrancy, the conductor who is rude to Helene Wright on the train, the three Irish boys who pick on Sula and Nel on their way home from school, the employers who refuse to hire Jude and Ajax because they're black, and the bargeman who finds Chicken Little's body, throws it into a burlap bag, and then ties the bag to the stern of his barge to protect his cargo of cloth from picking up any odor from the decaying corpse.

For the two days the boy's body is underwater, the bargeman wonders in disgust at the kind of parents who kill their children. And what do you make of the sheriff who suggests throwing Chicken Little back in the river? And how about the bargeman replying that he never should have taken the boy out of the water in the first place? By the time Chicken Little's body gets back to the Bottom, the only thing recognizable about the boy is his clothing. The people in the Bottom may be segregated from those in Medallion, but they can never escape their history or insulate themselves from the impact of the white dominant culture.

By the middle part of the twentieth century, the middle-class white people of Medallion want to escape from the capitalistic fallout that's overrun their Garden of Eden. They envision the area where the black people live as a suburb with a golf course. So the white people with money buy land from the black people in the Bottom and the black people use the money to purchase homes left by the white people in the valley. But Medallion is no longer the Promised Land, and the black people can't bring their sense of neighborhood with them because they've been dispersed among the houses of the poor whites who can't afford to move. In other words, the Bottom just doesn't wind up on the bottom; it ceases to exist. And that's not the worst of it. In falling prey to the lure of commercial success and material well-being, the people of the Bottom have exchanged what's important to them—their sense of family, tradition, and community—for jobs, money, and the false values of the capitalistic wasteland. The Bottom may have been far from perfect, but at least "it had been a place. Now there weren't any places left, just separate houses with separate televisions and separate telephones and less and less dropping by." What neither the Bottom dwellers nor the Medallion residents seem to realize is that it's the people who make the land, not the land that makes the people.

So what are the values that identify the Bottom as the Bottom? Though all support behavior that ensures the community's survival, some behaviors may have become outdated. Or perhaps not. Maybe it's the people who've lost touch with what the community needs to survive. Let's start with the men. We can see, for example, why it's probably not a good idea for a man living in a poor community like the Bottom to marry if he can't contribute in

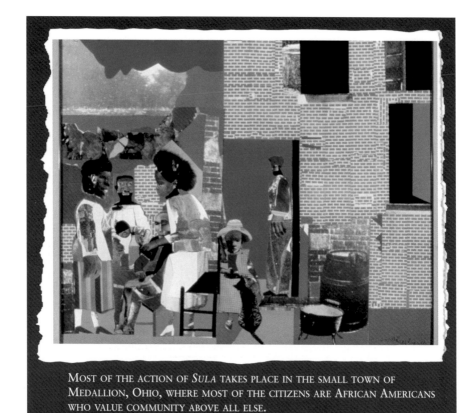

MOST OF THE ACTION OF *SULA* TAKES PLACE IN THE SMALL TOWN OF MEDALLION, OHIO, WHERE MOST OF THE CITIZENS ARE AFRICAN AMERICANS WHO VALUE COMMUNITY ABOVE ALL ELSE.

some significant ways to the support of his family. Or why, if he does plan to marry, it's helpful to have a job or an extended network of relatives and friends who can help him and his family in times of need. But none of the men in the Bottom seem to want to be tied down to a wife and kids even if they can contribute adequately to their support.

In avoiding their responsibilities, however, the men of the Bottom also limit their capacity for interdependency, intimacy, and spiritual growth. BoyBoy abandons his family, Jude moves out of his house, Ajax takes off for a tarmac where he can imagine himself as the black Charles Lindbergh, Tar Baby drowns himself in alcohol, Plum succumbs to drugs,

Shadrack urinates in front of women and children, and none of the "deweys" ever grows up enough to know what it's like to have an individual identity. All are so emotionally impoverished that marrying any one of them would be the mistake of a lifetime.

With the exception of Sula and Hannah, the women of the Bottom have a greater awareness of the need to care for others than the men. They seem to know that if the community is going to survive the inhuman treatment of the white dominant culture, they're going to have to stick together and help each other out. Even strong, independent Eva.

As accurate as Sula may be in pointing out the deficiencies of the community, the people of the Bottom cannot hear her insights because her actions speak louder than her words. And because she is so concerned with discovering and being true to who she thinks she is, she fails to develop any sense of empathy for others. Nel may kill her "Me" in her attempts to be conventional, but Sula falls far short of becoming a fully developed human being.

The people retaliate against the independent Sula by turning her into a scapegoat. When a little boy named Teapot trips coming down the stairs in front of her house, Sula is accused of pushing him. When another resident of the town chokes on a chicken bone while Sula happens to be walking by, everyone knows she's the cause of the man's death. But there isn't much they can do to Sula directly because she doesn't need or care much about them. None of the normal signs of vulnerability are apparent in her.

So the people protect themselves from the misfortunes brought upon their heads by Sula. The women love and cherish their husbands, the men spend more time repairing things around the house, and both take greater interests in their children in a community-wide attempt to band together against the devil in their midst who dares to be different. Isn't it ironic that "evil" Sula would be responsible for improving the quality of life for any

Bottom dweller who knew her? Why, you might ask, didn't they just run Sula out of town? The narrator tells us the people of the Bottom could kill easily if provoked, but they couldn't do it "by design." That wasn't their way. To do so was "not only unnatural, it was undignified. The presence of evil was something to be first recognized, then dealt with, survived, outwitted, triumphed over."

The community's triumph is also its great failure, however. Because the people of the Bottom were trying to be good for the wrong reason—in retaliation against Sula— they failed to benefit from the intrinsic worth of their own behavior. In other words, they never really became "good"; they remained a reaction to "bad" for as long as Sula lived. And whereas Sula's death in 1940 should have liberated them, it only made them search for another scapegoat, which they found in the tunnel being built under the river. Between 1927 and 1940, the tunnel represented hope, "the same hope that kept them picking beans for other farmers . . . kept them knee-deep in other people's dirt; kept them excited about other people's wars . . . kept them convinced that some magic 'government' was going to lift them up, out and away from that dirt, those beans, those wars."

In 1940, the tunnel turned from a hope for economic security and freedom from white reality to another unfulfilled promise. When the parading people of the Bottom look at the tunnel on National Suicide Day in 1941, all they see are the "teeth unrepaired, the coal credit cut off, the chest pains unattended, the school shoes unbought, the rush-stuffed mattresses, the broken toilets, the leaning porches, the slurred remarks and the staggering childish malevolence of their employers." In the same way that Nel realizes that Sula was her partner and not her problem, the community awakens to the fact that Sula was not the source of its misery either. And so they do to the tunnel what their codes of conventional behavior prohibited them from doing to Sula. They attack it and go bottom up in the flood that results.

In a weird sort of way, the community needed Sula more than she needed it. She was the one who kept them together and on the right path even if they were on it for the wrong reason. At least they were alive and happier than they had been before Sula returned from her ten-year walkabout. Now, what are their lives like in 1965? They've moved to the valley and are working at some of the service-industry jobs previously held by whites, but they've exchanged low incomes and cheap goods for people and a sense of belonging to something larger than themselves: a community.

Their material lives have improved, but what about their spiritual lives? How many years will it be before they start behaving like the white people in this novel? Do you think the train conductor who insults Helene Wright, the cop who throws Shadrack in jail, the Irish boys who torment Nel, the bargeman who finds Chicken Little's body, and the sheriff who suggests throwing the boy back in the river would have thought twice about running Sula out of town? They wouldn't have tolerated her mother for very long either. Rather than meld into a community that celebrates its own diversity, the people in the Bottom and the people from the valley, with the exception of a few poor whites, have mostly just switched places. For this reason, none of the citizens of either place receive any medals, and the bottom lines on the tombstones of those three marvelous but conflicted women keep ringing in our ears: PEACE, PEACE, PEACE!

The Narrative Structure

Sula begins with an ending and ends with a beginning. The large middle is divided into two parts. Each of the chapters in Part I is named after a year in the 1920s. These years focus on Sula and Nel when they are children, adolescents, and young women. All but one of the chapters in Part II are labeled by years in the late 1930s and early 1940s, when Sula and Nel are adults. Then there's a final year, 1965, in which Nel finally comes to understand and appreciate the best friend who died twenty-five years earlier. Woven into the lives of Nel and Sula are those of their family members and the people in the community where they live. These public dates don't just mark the private experiences that take place within them, however; they also serve as springboards of history as we watch Nel and Sula echo the behavior of their maternal ancestors. And what links all the people and all the years? Death. Almost every chapter opens with a death, or with death as its central focus. And like nature and racism, it cannot be avoided.

Morrison opens her novel in the latter part of the twentieth century with a description and history of the black community. The community, called the Bottom, is dead. The people who lived there have been displaced by the expanding city of Medallion. What was once a neighborhood where people sang, played banjos, wore colorful clothes, and had their hair done at Irene's Palace of Cosmetology to help ease the pain of living in a socially segregated and economically deprived community has now become a suburb of the hot and dusty streets that once were a fertile valley.

Enter Shadrack. It's 1919, and this is the first of eleven chapters designated by years. In the very first paragraph we read about Shadrack's devastating experience in World War I: He saw his comrade's head get blown off while running across a field toward enemy trenches. To focus and control his resulting fear of dying unexpectedly, Shadrack creates National Suicide Day, a day in which he and the people of the Bottom can purge themselves of their fears of sudden death through the ritual of an annual parade.

In 1920, Cecile Sabat is dying, and Nel is going with

her mother to the old woman's bedside in New Orleans. The trip becomes a vehicle for Morrison to tell us about Nel's family history, and we discover, in terms of the structure, that what happens in the chapters isn't restricted to the years the chapters are named after. We learn in this chapter, for example, that Nel's great-grandmother rescued her mother from the brothel in which she was born and raised her to be conventionally respectable. It is from her mother that Nel learns to value conformity for the sake of survival: hers, her family's, and her community's. But Nel doesn't want to be limited by the requirements needed to combat racism. She wants to be "Me" too. The sense of "Me" that Nel picked up after watching her mother be humiliated on the train ride to New Orleans opens her mind to the possibility of a friendship with the unconventional Sula.

You can see what Morrison is doing. She's using the years to frame events and provide the history we need to understand them. In 1921, Sula, her mom Hannah, and her grandmother Eva are living nontraditional lives in Eva's boardinghouse. We are introduced to their free-spirited, free-wheeling ways, but we also learn how single-parent Eva cut off her leg in 1895 to earn the money she needed to build the house that provides support for the Peace household. Eva is a tough Mother Goddess who can take life as well as give it. Before the chapter ends, we see her setting her son on fire to save him from himself.

In 1922, Nel and Sula are twelve years old and bonded to the point of being practically fused. What connects them forever is their responsibility—or failure to be responsible—in the death of Chicken Little. Now here's something interesting: Eva kills her son Plum in 1920, but we don't learn her reason until 1923, when Hannah asks Eva if she ever loved her children. That same year Hannah accidentally sets fire to herself and dies or is possibly killed by Eva in the ambulance on the way to the hospital. Also in the chapter "1923," Morrison introduces us to another way she uses time to convey narrative. Instead of relating chronologically the strange events leading up to Hannah's death, she starts with the second event first. Why? One reason may be because it is the event most likely to keep her readers engaged in the story. The opening line reads: "The second strange thing was Hannah's coming into her mother's room with an empty bowl and a peck of Kentucky Wonders and saying, 'Mama, did you ever love us?'" After the dramatic confrontation that follows between Hannah and Eva, the reader is more likely to be curious about the other events: the wind that didn't stop blowing, the dream of the red dress, and the odd behavior of Sula.

Part I of *Sula* ends on the positive, hopeful, upbeat note of Nel's marriage to Jude in 1927. It's the only chapter in this section where someone doesn't die! Nel's marriage, however, does sound the death knell for her friendship with Sula, who leaves the wedding reception and doesn't return to the Bottom for another ten years.

Part I examines what kinds of behavior in women the black community is willing to tolerate. Eva's leaving her children for eighteen months, Hannah's sleeping with any man she can get her hands on, and Sula's role in the death of Chicken Little may come first to mind. Part II focuses on what the community will not let women get away with, which is practically everything men are allowed to get away with. In Part I, the deaths are mostly physical; in Part II, they are mostly emotional. Part II also follows the structure laid out in Part I: Each chapter is designated by a year, time shifts among the years and within the years, and the novel ends on what may be as positive, hopeful, and upbeat a note as Morrison was capable of at this point in her writing career.

A plague of robins opens "1937" and welcomes Sula back to the Bottom. As participating readers, we're supposed to fill in the ten-year gap, but this one is bigger than the bridge that connects all the years in Part I and all but one of the years in Part II. On the other hand, the fact that Sula is pretty much the same person when she returns to the Bottom as when she left might mean that her experiences didn't count for much, that the more she experienced the more she remained the same. The same might be said about the town of Medallion: The years progress but social progress remains at a standstill.

Nevertheless, Sula doesn't waste a minute making up for lost time. In 1937, she "kills" the community's willingness to welcome her back to the Bottom by putting her grandmother "out" of the house and into a nursing home. She also drives a dagger into the heart of her friendship with Nel by having sex with her husband. In 1939, she drives the final nail into the community's coffin of tolerance by reportedly sleeping with white men and then

THIS YOUNG COUPLE MIGHT HAVE COME RIGHT OUT OF *SULA*.

attempts to nail Ajax with her newfound possessiveness. By 1940, she's dead at the age of thirty from what critic Barbara Christian calls "spiritual malnutrition."

Sula's death also terminates the role she played as the community's scapegoat. Without an evil in their midst to combat, the people of the Bottom no longer have a reason to care for one another. Nature reflects their new attitude. Frost comes early, Thanksgiving is lacking, and the promise of an early spring is wiped out when the celebrants of National Suicide Day die in their attempt to destroy the tunnel the white dominant culture would not allow them to help build. Any reader ready to toss in the towel of humankind, however, is saved by Eva, the life-giving Mother Goddess, who enables Nel to kill within herself the conventional wisdom she allowed to stunt her "Me" and be reborn into a new life that includes the memories, values, and spirit of her best friend Sula. Nel, finally, is both right and at peace.

The Title

Many critics wish Morrison had called her book *Nel* or *The Bottom* or almost anything other than *Sula*. The critics who favor *Nel* claim the story is really hers and should be named after her. They reason that Nel is the only character to change in any significant way, to experience any sense of self-realization. She not only moves beyond the limits of convention, she starts on the road to becoming a model for a new kind of black woman who is both free and responsible. The critics who prefer *The Bottom* for a title hold that Morrison's novel is really the history of a whole community and not just one person. They claim that if Sula was so important, Morrison would have opened the book with her. Instead, she opens with a description of the community, her dominant theme, followed by a chapter on Shadrack, who is at least as important to the people of the

Bottom as Sula. And unlike Shadrack, Sula doesn't even make it to the end of the book, dying two chapters and twenty-five years before Eva confronts Nel with her role in the death of Chicken Little.

Whether you think Sula is the main character in the novel or believe that the community is the central focus, there is no denying Morrison's extraordinary ability to create people who capture our imaginations and become a part of our lives long after we've finished reading one of her books. And while it is true that many of her characters live in a realm that often seems beyond real flesh and blood—think not only of Sula, Eva, and Hannah, but Pecola, Soaphead, and the three whores in *The Bluest Eye*—these almost mythic creatures contain an essence of truth about human nature that cannot be found in the events often paraded as facts in newspapers or in the clinical studies favored by those in the social sciences.

Morrison's creations cannot be reduced to the conclusions of a survey or the observations of a control group because they, like us, are complicated. They live in a gray area that science has not been able to penetrate. To underscore her efforts to create people who cannot be reduced to simple interpretations, Morrison also creates narrative structures that are expansive and diverse enough to contain the wide range of her characters' personalities and histories.

In other words, Morrison's books are not easy reads, but they are rewarding. Although her novels are anchored in African-American characters living in African-American communities, they are never "about" only the African-American experience any more than James Joyce's novels are only about Ireland. Like other great writers whose works make up the world's literary canon, Morrison's fictions transcend setting, race, class, and gender to help us better understand and appreciate the "human condition."

Chronology

1931
Chloe Anthony Wofford born at home on February 18 to George and Ramah Wofford in Lorain, Ohio. Second of four children.

1949
Graduates with honors from Lorain High School.

1953
Graduates with Bachelor of Arts degree from Howard University. Changes first name to Toni because people can't remember "Chloe."

1955
Graduates with Master of Arts degree from Cornell University. Teaches English at Texas Southern University in Houston.

1957
Teaches English at Howard University.

1958
Marries Harold Morrison, an architect from Jamaica.

1961
Gives birth to first son, Harold Ford.

1964
Divorces Harold Morrison; denied tenure at Howard University; returns to parents' home in Lorain, Ohio. Slade Kevin is born.

1965
Works as associate editor for the L. W. Singer Publishing Company in Syracuse, New York, a subsidiary of the Random House Publishing Company. *College Reading Skills* is published by Knopf.

1967
Promoted to senior editor at Random House Publishing Company in New York City. Begins first novel.

1970
The Bluest Eye is published by Holt, Rinehart & Winston.

1971
Teaches at the State University of New York (SUNY) at Purchase.

1973
Sula is published by Knopf.

1974
The Black Book, which Morrison edited, is published by Random House.

1975
Receives National Book Award nomination and Ohionana Book Award for *Sula*.

1976
Serves as Visiting Lecturer at Yale University until 1977.

1977
Song of Solomon published by Knopf. Receives National Book Critics Circle Award and American Academy and Institute of Arts and Letters Award. *Song of Solomon* named Book-of-the-Month Club Selection. Appointed to the National Council on the Arts by President Jimmy Carter.

1978
Featured on a segment of the Public Broadcasting System's television series "Writers in America."

1981
Tar Baby published by Knopf. Elected to the American Academy and Institute of Arts and Letters. Photograph appears on the cover of *Newsweek*.

1983
Leaves Random House. "Recitatif," Morrison's first short story, appears in *Confirmations: Stories by Black Women*, edited by Amiri and Amina Baraka and published by William Morrow.

1984
Accepts position as the Albert Schweitzer Professor of Humanities, State University of New York (SUNY) at Albany, 1984–1989.

1985
Receives New York State Governor's Arts Award.

1986
Teaches at Bard College until 1988. *Dreaming Emmett*, a play about Emmett Till, is produced in Albany.

1987
Beloved is published by Knopf. Nominated for National Book Award and National Book Critics Award. Main selection of Book of the Month Club. Regent's Lecturer at University of California at Berkeley and Santagata Lecturer at Bowdoin College.

1988
Wins the Pulitzer Prize for Fiction, the Melcher Award, the Before Columbus Foundation Award, and the Elizabeth

Cady Stanton Award from the National Organization for Women. Black writers and critics mount national protest when she does not receive the National Book Award.

1989
Named Robert F. Goheen Professor of Humanities at Princeton University, wins Modern Language Association of America's Commonwealth Award in Literature.

1990
Awarded Chianti Ruffino Antico Fattore International Literary Prize.

1992
Jazz published by Knopf in New York. *Playing in the Dark: Whiteness and the Literary Imagination*, a collection of literary criticism published by Harvard University Press. *Race-ing Justice, En-Gendering Power: Essays on Anita Hill, Clarence Thomas, and the Construction of Social Reality*, a collection of perspectives on the Clarence Thomas hearings regarding his nomination to the Supreme Court, published by Pantheon.

1993
Wins Nobel Prize in Literature.

1994
Awarded International Condorcet Chair at the École Normale Superieure and College de France. *The Nobel Lecture on Literature* published by Knopf.

1996
The Dancing Mind, Morrison's acceptance speech for the National Book Foundation Medal for Distinguished Contribution to American Letters, published by Knopf.

1997
Birth of a Nation'hood: Gaze, Script, and Spectacle in the

O. J. Simpson Case, co-edited with Claudia Brodsky Lacour, published by Pantheon.

1998
Paradise published by Knopf. Named A. D. White Professor at Large at Cornell University. Film adaptation of *Beloved*, starring Oprah Winfrey and Danny Glover, is released.

1999
The Big Box, a children's story co-authored with Slade Morrison, published by Hyperion.

2001
Toni Morrison Society hosts Morison's seventieth birthday celebration at New York Public Library on February 17.

2002
The Book of Mean People, with son Slade Morrison, published by Knopf.

2003
Love, Morrison's eighth novel, *The Ant or the Grasshopper?* published by Knopf and *The Lion or the Mouse?*, written with Slade, published by Knopf as part of the Who's Got Game series.

2004
The Poppy or the Snake?, with son Slade, published by Knopf.

2005
Awarded Coretta Scott King Book Award for *Remember: The Journey to School Integration*.

Works by Toni Morrison

Novels
The Bluest Eye (1970)
Sula (1973)
Song of Solomon (1977)
Tar Baby (1981)
Beloved (1987)
Jazz (1992)
Paradise (1998)
Love (2003)

Nonfiction
College Reading Skills (1965).

Playing in the Dark: Whiteness and the Literary Imagination (1992).

The Nobel Acceptance Speech (1994).

The Dancing Mind (1996) Acceptance Speech for National Book Foundation Medal for Distinguished Contribution to American Letters.

Drama
Dreaming Emmett (1985).

Works Edited or Co-authored
The Black Book (1974).

Race-ing Justice, En-gendering Power: Essays on Anita Hill, Clarence Thomas, and the Construction of Social Reality (1992)

Deep Sightings and Rescue Missions: Fiction, Essays, and Conversation (1996). Writings by Toni Cade Bambara.

Birth of a Nation'hood: Gaze, Script, and Spectacle in the O. J. Simpson Case (1997). Co-edited with Claudia Brodsky Lacour.

Essays and Short Stories
"What the Black Woman Thinks About Women's Lib," *New York Magazine* (August 22, 1971).

"Behind the Making of The Black Book," *Black World* (Feburary 1974).

"Rediscovering Black History," *New York Times Magazine* (August 11, 1974).

"Reading," *Mademoiselle* (May 1975).

"Slow Walk of Trees (as Grandmother Would Say) Hopeless as (Grandfather Would Say)," *New York Times Magazine* (July 4, 1976).

"City Limits, Village Values, Concepts of Neighborhood in Black Fiction," *Literature and the Urban Experience*. Ed. Jaye and Watts (1981).

"Recitatif," in *Confirmations: Stories by Black Women*. Ed. Baraka and Baraka (1983).

"Memory, Creation, and Writing," *Thought* (December 1984).

"Rootedness: The Ancestor as Foundation," in *Black Women Writers* (1950–1980). Ed. Evans (1984).

Notes

Quotations by Toni Morrison and information about her life are from the following interviews: Charlie Rose, "Toni Morrison," *The Charlie Rose Show* (May 1, 1993) PBS; Gloria Naylor, "A Conversation," *Southern Review*, New Series 21 (July 1985): 567–593; Christina Davis, "Interview with Toni Morrison," *Presence Africaine: Revue Culturelle du Monde Noir*, (1st Quarterly, 1988), reprinted in *Toni Morrison: Critical Perspectives Past and Present*, edited by Henry Louis Gates Jr. and K. A. Appiah (New York: Amistad 1993): 412–420; Nellie McKay, "An Interview with Toni Morrison," *Contemporary Literature*, 24 (Winter 1983): 413–429; Thomas LeClair, "'The Language Must Not Sweat,'" *New Republic*, 184 (March 21, 1981): 25–29; Jean Strouse, "Toni Morrison's Black Magic," *Newsweek*, March 30, 1981: 53–54; Robert B. Stepto, "'Intimate Things in Place': A Conversation with Toni Morrison," *Massachusetts Review*, 18 (Autumn 1977): 473–489; and Mel Watkins, "A Talk with Toni Morrison," *The New York Times Book Review* (September 11, 1977): 48, 50.

Further Information

Further Reading

Books
Bloom, Harold. *Toni Morrison*. Bloom's Major Novelists Series. New York: Chelsea House, 1999.

_____. *Toni Morrison*. Bloom's BioCritiques Series. New York: Chelsea House, 2002.

Haskins, Jim. *Toni Morrison: Telling a Tale Untold*. Brookfield, CT: Millbrook Press, 2002.

Rhodes, Lisa Renee. *Toni Morrison: Great American Writer*. Danbury, CT: Franklin Watts, Inc., 2001.

Film Adaptation
Beloved (1998). Starring Oprah Winfrey, Danny Glover.

Video Recordings
Four Girls and Toni Morrison. Landmark Media, 1994.

Identifiable Qualities: Toni Morrison. Corentyne Productions, 1989.

"Toni Morrison." *In Black and White*. Part 3. Six Profiles of African-American Authors series. RTSI Swiss TV/California Newsreel, 1992.

"Toni Morrison with A. S. Byatt." *Writers Talk: Ideas of Our Time* series. ICA Video, 1989.

"A Writer's Work with Toni Morrison." *World of Ideas with Bill Moyers*. PBS Video, 1990.

Web Sites

www.luminarium.org/contemporary/tonimorrison
(includes all known web sources).

www.gradesaver.com/ClassicNotes/Authors/about_toni_
morrison.html (includes special section on *The Bluest Eye*).

www.tcom.ohiou.edu/books/morrison.htm (discussion of
community as character in Morrison's novels).

www.az.com/~andrads/morrison/eye.html
(discussion of *The Bluest Eye*).

www.atrium.com/names/name-tibu.html
(reader's road map to the novels).

www.english.uwosh.edu?henson/281/eyeque1.html (study
questions for *The Bluest Eye*).

www.readinggroupguides.com/guides/bluest_eye_author
(reading guide to *The Bluest Eye* for group discussions).

www.cqu.edu.au/arts/humanites/litstud/
naff/naffch9morrison.html (introduction to *The Bluest Eye*).

www.210.pair.com/udticg/lessonplans/sula/
(themes of love and death in *Sula*).

www.umass.edu/complit/acplanet/morrison.html
(discussion questions for *Sula*).

www.goodbookslately.com/recommendedbooks/guides/
sula. shtml (discussion of themes in *Sula*).

All Web sites accessed July 8, 2004.

Bibliography

Awkward, Michael. "'The Evil of Fulfillment': Scapegoating and Narration in *The Bluest Eye*." In *Toni Morrison: Critical Perspectives Past and Present*, edited by Henry Louis Gates Jr., and K. A. Appiah, pp. 175–209. New York: Amistad, 1993.

_____. "Roadblocks and Relatives: Critical Revision in Toni Morrison's *The Bluest Eye*." In *Critical Essays on Toni Morrison*, edited by Nellie McKay, pp. 57–68. Boston: Hall, 1988.

Baker Jr., Houston A. "When Lindbergh Sleeps with Bessie Smith: The Writing of Place in *Sula*." In *Toni Morrison: Critical Perspectives Past and Present*, edited by Henry Louis Gates Jr., and K. A. Appiah, pp. 236–261. New York: Amistad, 1993.

Beaulieu, Elizabeth Ann, ed. *The Toni Morrison Encyclopedia*. Westport, CT: Greenwood Press, 2003.

Blackburn, Sarah. "*Sula*." *The New York Times Book Review* (December 30, 1973). Reprinted in *Toni Morrison: Critical Perspectives Past and Present*, edited by Henry Louis Gates Jr., and K. A. Appiah, pp. 6–8. New York: Amistad, 1993.

Bloom, Harold, ed. *Toni Morrison*. New York: Chelsea House, 1990.

_____. ed. Toni Morrison's *The Bluest Eye*. New York: Chelsea House, 1999.

Bryant, Jerry H. "Sula." *The Nation* (July 6, 1974). Reprinted in *Toni Morrison: Critical Perspectives Past and Present*, edited by Henry Louis Gates Jr., and K. A. Appiah, pp. 8–10. New York: Amistad, 1993.

Butler-Evans, Elliott. *Race, Gender, and Desire: Narrative Strategies in the Fiction of Toni Cade Bambara, Toni Morrison, and Alice Walker*. Philadelphia: Temple University, 1989.

Byerman, Keith E. "Beyond Realism." In *Toni Morrison: Critical Perspectives Past and Present*, edited by Henry Louis Gates Jr., and K. A. Appiah, pp. 100–125. New York: Amistad, 1993.

_____. "Intense Behaviors: The Use of the Grotesque in *The Bluest Eye* and *Eva's Man*." *CLA Journal* 25 (June 1984): 447–457.

Christian, Barbara. "Community and Nature: The Novels of Toni Morrison." *The Journal of Ethnic Studies* 7 (Winter 1980): 65–78.

_____. "The Contemporary Fables of Toni Morrison." In *Toni Morrison: Critical Perspectives Past and Present*, edited by Henry Louis Gates Jr., and K. A. Appiah, New York: Amistad, 1993.

Duvall, John N. *The Identifying Fictions of Toni Morrison: Modernist Authenticity and Postmodern Blackness*. New York: Palgrave & St. Martin's Press, 2000.

Earle, Kathryn. "Teaching Controversy: *The Bluest Eye* in the Multicultural Classroom." In *Approaches to Teaching the Novels of Toni Morrison*, edited by Nellie McKay and Kathryn Earle, pp. 27–33. New York: The Modern Language Association, 1997.

Eckard, Paula Gallant. *Maternal Body and Voice in Toni Morrison, Bobbie Ann Mason, and Lee Smith.* Columbia: University of Missouri 2002.

Eichelberger, Julia. *Prophets of Recognition: Ideology and the Individual in Novels by Ralph Ellison, Toni Morrison, Saul Bellow, and Eudora Welty.* Baton Rouge: Louisiana State University, 1999.

Feng, Pin-chia. *The Female Bildungsroman by Toni Morrison and Maxine Hong Kingston: A Postmodern Reading.* New York: Peter Lang, 1998.

Fick, Thomas H., and Eva Gold. "Authority, Literacy, and Modernism in *The Bluest Eye*." In *Approaches to Teaching the Novels of Toni Morrison*, edited by Nellie McKay and Kathryn Earle, pp. 56–62. New York: The Modern Language Association, 1997.

Frankel, Haskel. "*The Bluest Eye*." *The New York Times Book Review* (November 1, 1970). Reprinted in *Toni Morrison: Critical Perspectives Past and Present*, edited by Henry Louis Gates Jr., and K. A. Appiah, pp. 3–4. New York: Amistad, 1993.

Furman, Jan. *Toni Morrison's Fiction.* Columbia: University of South Carolina, 1996.

Gates, Henry Louis Jr., and K.A. Appiah, eds. *Toni Morrison: Critical Perspectives Past and Present.* New York: Amistad, 1993.

Gibson, Donald B. "Text and Contertext in *The Bluest Eye*." In *Toni Morrison: Critical Perspectives Past and Present*, edited by Henry Louis Gates Jr., and K. A. Appiah, pp. 159–174. New York: Amistad, 1993.

Gillespie, Diane, and Missy Dehn Kubitshek. "Who Cares? Women-Centered Psychology in *Sula*." In *Toni Morrison's Contemporary Criticism*, edited by David Middleton, pp. 61–94. New York: Garland, 2000.

Grewal, Gurleen. *Circles of Sorrow, Lines of Struggle*. Baton Rouge: Louisiana State University, 1998.

_____. "'Laundering the Head of Whitewash': Mimicry and Resistance in *The Bluest Eye*." In *Approaches to Teaching the Novels of Toni Morrison*, edited by Nellie McKay and Kathryn Earle, pp. 118–126. New York: The Modern Language Association.

Hatch, Shari Dorantes. "Morrison, Toni." *African-American Writers: A Dictionary*, edited by Shari Dorantes Hatch and Michael R. Strickland, pp. 257–260. Santa Barbara, CA: ABC-CLIO, 2000.

Heinze, Denise. *The Dilemma of "Double-Consciousness" in Toni Morrison's Novels*. Athens: University of Georgia, 1993.

_____. "Toni Morrison." *Dictionary of Literary Biography: American Novelists Since World War II*, 3rd Series, Vol.143, edited by James R. Giles and Wanda H. Giles, pp. 171–187. Washington, DC: Bruccoli Clark, 1994.

Higgins, Therese E. *Religiosity, Cosmology, and Folklore: The African Influence in the Novels of Toni Morrison*. New York: Routledge, 2001.

Hirsch, Marianne. "Maternal Narratives: 'Cruel Enough to Stop the Blood.'" In *Toni Morrison: Critical Perspectives Past and Present*, edited by Henry Louis Gates Jr,. and K. A. Appiah, pp. 261–273. New York: Amistad, 1993.

Holloway, Karla F. C., and Stephanie A. Demetrakopoulos. *New Dimensions of Spirituality: A Biracial and Bicultural Reading of the Novels of Toni Morrison*. New York: Greenwood, 1987.

hooks, bell. *Black Looks: Race and Representation*. Boston: South End Press, 1992.

House, Elizabeth B., "*Sula*: Imagery, Figurative Language, and Symbols." In *Approaches to Teaching the Novels of Toni Morrison*, edited by Nellie McKay and Kathryn Earle, pp. 99–105. New York: The Modern Language Association, 1997.

Hurston, Zora Neale. "My People! My People!" *Mother Wit and the Laughing Barrell*, ed. Alan Dundes, pp. 23–33. Englewood Cliffs, NJ: Prentice-Hall, 1973.

Lubiano, Wahneema. "Toni Morrison." In *African-American Writers*, 2nd edition, Vol., 2, pp. 581–597. New York: Scribners, 2001.

McDowell, Deborah E. "'The Self and the Other': Reading Toni Morrison's *Sula* and the Black Female Text." In *Critical Essays on Toni Morrison*, edited by Nellie McKay, pp. 77–90. Boston: Hall, 1988.

McKay, Nellie, and Kathryn Earle, eds. *Approaches to Teaching the Novels of Toni Morrison*. New York: The Modern Language Association, 1997.

Middleton, David, ed. *Toni Morrison's Fiction: Contemporary Criticism*. New York: Garland, 2000.

Morrison, Toni. *The Bluest Eye*. Boston: Holt, Rinehart and Winston, 1970.

_____. *Sula*. New York: Alfred A. Knopf, 1973.

_____. *The Nobel Lecture in Literature*. New York: Alfred A. Knopf, 1994.

_____. "Unspeakable Things Unspoken: The Afro-American Presence in American Literature." *Michigan Quarterly Review* (Winter 1989): 1–34.

Otten, Terry. *The Crime of Innocence in the Fiction of Toni Morrison*. Columbia: University of Missouri, 1989.

Perez-Torres, Rafael. "Tracing and Erasing: Race and Pedagogy in *The Bluest Eye*." In *Approaches to Teaching the Novels of Toni Morrison*, edited by Nellie McKay and Kathryn Earle, pp. 21–26. New York: The Modern Language Association, 1997.

Powell, Timothy. "Toni Morrison: The Struggle to Depict the Black Figure on the White Page." In *Toni Morrison's Fiction: Contemporary Criticism*, edited by David Middleton, pp. 45–60. New York: Garland, 2000.

Ranveer, Kashinath. *Black Feminist Consciousness*. Jaipur (India): Printwell, 1995.

Rosenberg, Ruth. "Seeds in Hard Ground: Black Girlhood in *The Bluest Eye*." *Black American Literature Forum* 21 (Winter 1987): 435–445.

Rubenstein, Roberta. "Pariahs and Community." In *Toni Morrison: Critical Perspectives Past and Present*, edited by Henry Louis Gates Jr. and K. A. Appiah, pp. 126–158. New York: Amistad 1993.

Samuels, Wilfred D., and Clenora Hudson-Weems. *Toni Morrison*. Boston: Twayne 1990.

Sissman, L. E. "*The Bluest Eye.*" *The New Yorker* (January 23, 1971). Reprinted in *Toni Morrison: Critical Perspectives Past and Present*, edited by Henry Louis Gates, Jr. and K. A. Appiah, pp. 4–5. New York: Amistad, 1993.

Spillers, Hortense J. "A Hateful Passion, a Lost Love." In *Toni Morrison: Critical Perspectives Past and Present*, edited by Henry Louis Gates Jr. and K. A. Appiah, pp. 210–235. New York: Amistad, 1993.

Tate, Claudia. "Toni Morrison." In *Black Women Writings at Work*, edited by Claudia Tate, pp. 117–131. New York: Continuum, 1983.

Tirrell, Lynne. "Storytelling and Moral Agency." In *Toni Morrison's Fiction: Contemporary Criticism*, edited by David Middleton, pp. 3–26. New York: Garland, 2000.

Weever, Jacqueline ed. "The Inverted World of Toni Morrison's *The Bluest Eye* and Sula." *CLA Journal* 22 (1979): 402–414.

Wilentz, Gay. "An African-Based Reading of Sula." In *Approaches to Teaching the Novels of Toni Morrison*, edited by Nellie McKay and Kathryn Earle, pp. 127–134. New York: The Modern Language Association, 1997.

Willis, Susan. "Eruptions of Funk: Historicizing Toni Morrison." In *Modern Critical Interpretations: The Bluest Eye*, edited by Harold Bloom, pp. 45–64. New York: Chelsea House, 1999.

Bibliographies

Alexander, Harriet. "Toni Morrison: An Annotated Bibliography of Critical Articles and Essays, 1975–1984." *College Language Association Journal*, 33 (September 1989): 81–93.

Fikes, Robert, Jr. "Echoes from Small Town Ohio: A Toni Morrison Bibliography." *Obsidian* 5 (Spring–Summer 1979): 142–148.

Martin, Curtis. "A Bibliography of Writings by Toni Morrison." In *Contemporary Women Writers: Narrative Strategies*, edited by Catherine Rainwater and William J. Scheick, pp. 205–207. Lexington: University Press of Kentucky, 1985.

Index

Page numbers in **boldface** are illustrations, tables, and charts.
Fictional characters are shown with a (c).

About the Author

Richard Andersen, a former Fulbright Professor, Karolyi Foundation Fellow, and James Thurber Writer in Residence, currently teaches writing and literature at Springfield College in Springfield, Massachusetts. In 2003, Springfield College nominated him for the Carnegie Foundation's United States Professor of the Year Award. His more than twenty books include six on writing, five novels, four critical studies, a biography, and an examination of contemporary education. *Toni Morrison* and *Arthur Miller*, two of the first entries in the Writers and Their Works series, are his first books for Marshall Cavendish Benchmark.